BEFORE THE

Legend

BEFORE THE

Legend

THE RISE OF
BOB MARLEY

CHRISTOPHER JOHN FARLEY

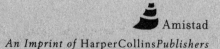
Amistad
An Imprint of HarperCollinsPublishers

FOR SHARON, DYLAN, AND EMMA—
HIGH TIDE OR LOW TIDE

The Library of Congress has cataloged the hardcover edition as follows:

Farley, Christopher John.
    Before the legend: the rise of Bob Marley / Christopher John Farley.—1st ed.
        p. cm.
    ISBN: 978-0-06-053991-7
    ISBN-10: 0-06-053991-7
        1. Marley, Bob. 2. Reggae musicians—Jamaica—Biography.

    ML420.M3313 F37 2006
    782.421646092 B 22

                                                                2006042743

ISBN: 978-0-06-053992-4 (pbk.)
ISBN-10: 0-06-053992-5

07 08 09 10 11 BVG /RRD 10 9 8 7 6 5 4 3 2 1

CONTENTS

STIR IT UP

In the summer of 2005, I traveled to the town in which Bob Marley was born in order to see the place where he was buried. Marley's hometown is Nine Miles, Jamaica, a small village in the parish of St. Ann that is a three-hour car ride from the capital city of Kingston. Getting there is a hilly, winding drive, and the road, at times, is about one and a half lanes across, forcing drivers to play periodic games of chicken with various vehicles—cars, buses, trucks laden with day laborers—speeding down the slopes in the opposite direction. I was born in Kingston, but I left the island when I was young and I can't do many basic Jamaican-y things. I can't, for example, tell you a single thing about the rules of cricket. I don't speak with a Jamaican accent and I can't fake one convincingly. I can't drive on the left on hilly twisty roads. I pressed on anyway. I had arranged a meeting in Nine Miles with Cedella Marley Booker, Bob's mother. She had grown reclusive in recent years and gave very few interviews. But Chris Blackwell, one of Marley's producers and the founder of Island Records, interceded on my behalf, and Mother Booker agreed to grant me an audience. At this point, I had been working on a book about Marley's life for several years. I had interviewed Marley's family members, friends, and fellow musicians. I had unearthed crumbling old print interviews of Marley and listened to scratchy home recordings he had made but never released. I had visited his old haunts in Trench Town and throughout Kingston. I had been given unreleased recordings of the Wailers conversing in the studio so I could get insight into how they created their music. Now I wanted to finish my book where it had all started, and where it had all ended as well.

This is a book about beginnings. The period before fame arrives is the time when most artists collect the raw life stuff that will form the core of their work. Once a musician starts writing about how hard life is on the road, and the predation of the paparazzi, it's generally over. He has lost touch with the real experiences that connect ordinary listeners to his music. In many if not most cases, an artist's initial years of struggle represent the most interesting period of his or her career. Music legends often end their lives in strikingly similar circumstances—burdened by celebrity, hooked on drugs, haunted by the inability to live up to the greatness of earlier work. Fame can homogenize an artist, blurring parts of his identity so critics can slot him into pop cultural trends or the public can use him to fill national psychic needs. Or fame can caricature a star, exaggerating his original characteristics into something cartoony, grotesque, and sometimes unrecognizable as human. Bob Marley died young, but he managed to avoid many of the most common pitfalls and pratfalls of rock martyrdom. Marley once opined: "If something can corrupt you, you're corrupted already." He was not a drug addict (unless you count ganja). He did not die broke (though his money was poorly managed during his lifetime). And he was not all that conflicted about success (he used to joke to journalists that he drove a BMW because it stood for Bob Marley and the Wailers). He lived and died for music, but in the end it was not music that killed him.

Marley's struggle started early. His bandmate Peter Tosh made secret autobiographical recordings called the "Red X" tapes. I was given access to parts of those tapes that have never been published. On them, Tosh discusses the obstacles that stood in his way, and in Bob's way, when they were young. "I began to realize that I was coming in close confrontation with devils daily in the flesh," Tosh says. "I realized that hell is not down yonder, but right here among men. . . . But I never fear the devil."

Bob's early, dry seasons forced him to put down deep roots. "Yeah, mon, let me tell you something 'bout me," Marley said during a visit to Philadelphia in 1979. "You see me—Negro in a sufferin' environment. I don't know how to live good. I only know how to suffer. You unnerstan? So anywhere you see me, I'm sufferin' all the while. Me don't really change . . . What is big life to some people, that is not what I call life. What I call life is I wake up and drink a likkle fish tea. Me don't know about the big life."

Blackwell recalls stopping by an upscale store in St. Martin with Marley during a world tour in 1980. It was one of the few times he ever saw Marley become furious. Inside the store, the proprietors questioned whether Marley had the money to buy their goods. When he promptly produced a wad of cash, he was interrogated about whether he had stolen it. Meanwhile, in the street, a crowd of fans had gathered to catch a glimpse of the reggae star. "Inside the store he was a thief," says Blackwell. "Outside, he was a hero."

Marley's mother is black, his father accepted as white. Very little had been known about the "white" side of Marley's family when I started this biography. The "white" part of Marley's family tree had been dismissed as fallen leaves—tattered remnants of another season, and not worth chasing. It is unclear in every book published on the singer whether Marley's father was Jamaican or British or even exactly how old he was. Even Bob's mother was foggy on key facts about her husband. My research, however, led me to relatives on Marley's father's side of the family. Chris Marley, a great-nephew of Bob's father, has served as a kind of family historian over the years. He has spent hundreds of hours researching his ties to Bob and was kind enough to share some of what he had found with me. Bob Marley once told Chris, "My father was a ship's captain," but Chris later learned that tale was untrue. "[Bob's father] was a bit of an adventurer and a rebel," says Chris. Thanks to his research and documentation, I was able to find out where Marley's father was born, his age, and details about his military service.

In previous accounts of Marley's upbringing, half his life is missing. Information about Marley's "white" father is critically important in understanding Marley's expansive cultural viewpoint on the world. Bob Marley once said: "If you're white and you're wrong, then you're wrong, if you're black and you're wrong, you're wrong. People are people. Black, blue, pink, green—God make no rules about color, only society make rules where my people suffer and that why we must have redemption and redemption now."

Even when he was singing about revelation and revolution, or vampires sucking the blood of the sufferers, or buffalo soldiers stolen from Africa, there was something redemptive, something sunny, about Marley's outlook. Marley once said: "I don't think of Third World. To me, I am of the First World. I can't put people in classes." He was always seeking to bring people together rather than to divide them. On another occasion he declared: "There is no right or left. We go straight ahead." That's part of why Marley's music is embraced all around the world, by people of disparate economic, political, and social circumstances: rude boys and frat boys, soccer moms and stockbrokers, rebel leaders and captains of industry. Marley was a smiling revolutionary, and the rhythmic and melodic affability of his music made his insurgent message go down easy. There was a charming playfulness about Marley that was always evident in his music and in the way he carried himself in life, and even in how he approached death. "I don't believe in death neither in flesh nor in spirit," Marley once said.

Marley's primary producer told me a haunting story about him. Marley and Blackwell, although they worked together for a decade, were almost never photographed together. They both agreed that if they were pictured in the same frame, there would be those, confronted with their contrasting skin tones, who would falsely assume that the white producer must be the real master-mind behind the black musician's music. So when they were to-gether, they avoided the cameras. But sometime in 1981, Marley, a photographer in tow, stopped by to see Blackwell and an-nounced that he had cancer. As shock registered on Blackwell's face, Marley asked the photographer to take a picture of them. It's the only picture Blackwell says he has of himself with Marley. In the face of death, Marley was looking for a laugh.

Marley's oldest daughter, Cedella, told me that near the end of his life, when his dreadlocks had begun to fall out because of the cancer treatments, he would still summon the strength to play with his kids. He would put on a Frankenstein mask from off the kitchen counter and chase his sons and daughters around their house in Miami. "A lot of people know Dad the musician," Ce-della says. "We've always known him as Dad—who could be corny, funny, serious at times, but would never spank. If he saw a tear in your eye, he would look the other way. That's the person that we know."

The Jamaican-American novelist Colin Channer once told me

that Marley's music provided a model not just for Caribbean musicians, but also for poets and prose writers, because in his songs, the sexual, the political, and the spiritual were able to intertwine without contradiction. He was a warrior and a peacemaker, a romantic and a realist, a high priest who could bend down low. Why was Marley so adroit at moving between moods, traveling between worlds, finding that natural mystic blowing through the air? The answer lies in the beginning. The early part of Marley's life—before the big-money record deals, before the beauty-pageant-winning girlfriends, before the covers of *High Times* and *Rolling Stone*, before the dreadlocks and the dread talk—offers up the most telling clues. In his childhood, he forged the friendships that formed the foundation for his music career. In his youth, he constructed the philosophy that informed his musical outlook. And during this early period, he developed the drive that would make him a superstar.

Marley wrote many of his finest and most famous songs—including "One Love," "Stir It Up," "Lively Up Yourself," "Concrete Jungle"—in the 1960s when he was in his early twenties. Says Danny Sims, who produced the Wailers' material between 1967 and 1972: "From 1967 until he died, I don't think he wrote ten songs. He might have finished the songs. He might have added a verse here and there. But every song that you hear, Bob had before we met him." Blackwell disputes Sims's take on Bob's output. "You know how I know that's not true? I saw him write new songs," argues Blackwell. But Blackwell agrees that Bob drew on his early songwriting throughout his recording career. "Bob felt that he hadn't gotten paid what he should have for his early songs because producers ripped him off. I gave him the idea that for every new record he did, he could re-record some of his old songs that hadn't gotten a wider release." And so this biography is a portrait of the artist as a young man, before the man became a

star, and the star became a legend, and the legend became
shrouded by myth.

On my way to Nine Miles to see Mother Booker, I stopped in
to see Bunny Wailer. Bunny is the last surviving member of the
original, core Wailers trinity. Marley died of cancer in Miami in
1981. Peter Tosh was shot dead during an attack on his Kingston
home in 1987. Now only Bunny is left. A few associates of the
Wailers in their heyday had warned me against speaking with
Bunny. Blackwell told me that the real Bunny was long gone.
"That's not Bunny," he told me. "That's the devil in Bunny's body."
Others told me that Bunny would never talk to me. When Timothy White wrote his biography of Bob Marley, *Catch a Fire*
(1983), he thanked Bunny in his opening acknowledgments. But
Bunny says he refused to speak to White for the book, as he had
refused many other would-be interviewers over the years. Bunny
had long been known as the most spiritual member of what had
been a very mystical group. If Bob was Paul, and Peter was John,
Bunny was George. (There was no Ringo in the Wailers, though,
as we'll find out, there may have been a Yoko.) When Bunny
dropped out of the Wailers in 1974, he retreated to Jamaica and
out of the lidless gaze of international publicity.

The first time I talked to Bunny on the phone, he seemed full
of rage. He spoke loudly, and the phone crackled with distortion,
as if the international telecommunications lines could not contain
his passion. His voice, so guava sweet when singing, is low and
ragged when speaking—when he talks, he has the resonant, ring-
ing tones one would expect to emanate from a burning bush.
Bunny questioned my background, my motivation, my methods.
He wondered aloud if I was knowledgeable enough, if I was mature enough, and if I was Jamaican enough to write a book about
the Wailers. (I actually wondered the same things myself, but
hadn't given voice to them.) Bunny hinted that he would have to

be paid for his efforts, and suggested that I, like so many producers and record promoters had done in the past, was scamming the Wailers—he called it "scanning." The word *scanning* is an interesting coinage: it suggested that I was a clerk at a supermarket, handling him like a product from the frozen-food aisle, passing my laser beam over him, searching for a product bar code. I didn't challenge Bunny, I merely listened. He had decades of frustration—perhaps even four hundred years' worth—to unload and I wanted to give him his chance to express himself. Plus, I was intimidated. The Wailers were a reggae Mount Rushmore. Being castigated by Bunny was like being chewed out by a giant stone head. Bunny railed against the pirates who were bootlegging Wailers recordings around the world and against the recording companies that were making money off Wailers recordings without paying what he saw as adequate compensation to the musicians who had made the music in the first place. But slowly the interrogation became a conversation. By the end of our initial talk, Bunny had mellowed, and another side of the reggae great came out. He was wise, witty, friendly. And he agreed to speak again. So our dialogue continued, until we were talking on a regular basis, and not only about my book. We talked about the state of the music industry, his recording schedule, even the beauty of Jamaican women. He promised to introduce me to some "big-bottomed" island girls. I told him I was married. He told me that wouldn't be a problem.

Bunny told me where his house was, but didn't give me the exact street address. When I arrived, I realized why he didn't have to get specific. His gate was painted the Rasta colors of red, gold, and green, and adorned with the images of golden Ethiopian lions. At the center of the gate was the Wailers' crest: three hands interlocked in a triangle of strength, brotherhood, and solidarity. "The three hands that symbolize 'Tuff Gong' on the label each symbolize one of us, the original Wailers," Peter Tosh once said. "We did pledge as a group to continue the work of Rastafari, whatever happen." There were two garbage cans out in front of Bunny's house—and they, too, were painted red, gold, and green. Even his refuse was Rasta. Bunny came to the gate and opened it. He smiled broadly when he saw me and started laughing. "You're an Ethiopian brother!" he said. "I thought you were white!" We had talked only on the phone before.

Bunny shook my hand and ushered me through his gates. In the courtyard, there was a basketball hoop, a small banana tree, and two large empty speaker casings. Just inside the door to his house, there was a stationary bike. A sign posted on the wall read PLEASE LEAVE YOUR SHOES AT THE DOOR. Another sign read: REMEMBER: WHEN YOU COME HERE. WHAT YOU SEE HERE. WHAT YOU DO HERE. WHAT YOU HEAR HERE. WHEN YOU LEAVE HERE. LET IT STAY HERE. OR DON'T COME BACK HERE. This rather intimidating warning was next to a large poster of Goofy and Mickey Mouse in Rasta garb under a headline that read JAMAICA. Standing in the sunlight in his courtyard, Bunny spoke of his love of nature. He said he'd recorded much of his first solo album, *Blackheart Man*, while living "in the bush." He said he had heard a story of a woman who lived in the country and played the album repeatedly, only to come home one day after an extended period away to find that the bush had completely overrun her house. Because Bunny had made the album while in the wild, it had a magical connection to plant life. Declared Bunny of the incident: "Bunny Wailer music not just songs. Bunny Wailer music plant food!"

As we sat in Bunny's office, he called for some lunch—ackee and callaloo—and began to tell me tales about Bob Marley. Bunny's dreadlocks were tucked inside a large leather cap, and even inside the shaded room, he kept on his wide brown wraparound sunglasses. The walls of his office were adorned with mementos from the Wailers' heyday: albums, photos, newspaper clippings. Scattered on Bunny's small wooden desk were several black CDs, a boxed set of Bunny's solo work, and a photo of Ethiopian emperor Haile Selassie, who is revered as a god by Rastafari. Bunny took out a wooden pipe, stuffed it with herb, and fired it up. The room soon filled with smoke, and my head was soon filled with stories. Later, Bunny sent me a priceless treasure trove of information about the Wailers: more than seven hours' worth of audio recordings he had compiled that documented the early history of the band.

Mother Marley's home was my next stop. Her house was on a knoll overlooking the town. A small industry has built up around the property, which was Bob's childhood home, and guides lead travelers from all over the world on tours around the grounds. Mother Marley is a striking woman, and on that day she looked like Caribbean royalty. She was clad in a purple patterned headdress and matching robe. Her dark eyes seemed to stare past you even when she was talking directly to you. There was a sense of calm around her, like the cool shadowy air that precedes a warm rain. By some accounts, she seems to have passed this particular aura down to Bob. She was quiet at first, and remained seated throughout our conversation. She wanted to hear me talk. She asked me about my family, my feelings about Jamaica, my thoughts about children. I didn't tell her that my wife and I had discussed naming our son Marley, but ultimately decided against it because Marley Farley would have sounded ridiculous. Instead I told her that my three-year-old son (whom we named Dylan) was already a Bob Marley fan, and would sing and dance to his music whenever he heard it. She laughed. "From an early age, children know him," she said. "They don't know him, but they know him."

I later went to see Bob's mausoleum, which is only a few paces away. Marley, as it turns out, is not buried beneath the ground, but six feet above the earth in a tomb made of marble imported from Ethiopia. Around the tomb are some of the gifts that pilgrims have left him over the many years: a worn soccer ball, a homemade guitar, a painting of Marcus Garvey. On the ledge of the tomb is a Bible, opened to the Twenty-third Psalm:

Yea, though I walk through the valley of the shadow of death, I will fear no evil: for thou art with me; thy rod and thy staff comfort me.

Mother Marley told me I should come back to visit her in Jamaica again. "I live here and in Miami," she said, "but as I get older I find myself spending more time here. It's home—that's what it is." Much of this book, because it is about Marley, is also about Jamaica. Marley told a Jamaican magazine in 1978: "Well, is the people of Jamaica really make me what I am. Is them say 'Go Bob' . . . I sing, the people applaud. Them people down here is the greatest people in the world. Is them build I and I." Jamaica is a place that goes by many names. It has been called "The Land of Wood and Water" and "The Land of Look Behind." Columbus deemed it "the fairest island that eyes have beheld" and listed it as Yamaye in a log entry in 1493. The Indians who were among the first inhabitants of the island called it Xaymaica and other variations; Spanish invaders called the place Santiago. But after the British took over the island in 1655, one name took hold: Jamaica. Marley, like the land of his birth, was also a man of many identities. His family called him Nesta—his original first name, which his mother replaced with Bob when she emigrated to America for a brief period in Marley's youth. He also was called the Skipper, for his commanding nature, and the Tuff Gong, for his fortitude. In his songs, he referred to himself as the Duppy Conquerer (for his power over the spirit world), the Small Axe (who can chop down the big tree). For a time, disillusioned by his struggles in the Jamaican music industry, he lived in Wilmington,

Delaware, and worked in an auto plant where few of his fellow employees knew his true background or his real name. He later returned to Jamaica and became a superstar, embracing the name by which the world now knows him: Bob Marley.

For many people, Marley isn't a ghost; he isn't just a voice on the radio or a face on a T-shirt. He's an active presence in their lives and the symbol of something relevant and important. When I talked to Alan "Skill" Cole, one of Bob's best friends and the Wailers' former manager, he talked about Bob in the present tense, as if Bob were still on tour, in the studio—or in the next room. When Bono, lead singer for the Irish rock band U2, inducted Marley into the Rock and Roll Hall of Fame in 1994, he said this about the reggae great: "He wanted everything at the same time and was everything at the same time: prophet, soul rebel, Rastaman, herbsman, wild man, a natural mystic man, ladies' man, island man, family man, Rita's man, soccer man, showman, shaman, human, Jamaican." In 2001, I interviewed Bob Dylan, and our conversation turned to Marley and his songwriting. Marley held Dylan in the highest regard, and seemed to understand his cryptic lyrics in a way that went beyond other listeners. "I like Dylan's music. He really say it clear," Marley once said. "Come from da same place. Yeah, mus'. Maybe I'll give him inspiration." In my talk with Dylan, I said that Marley's music was proof that political songwriting could have long-term impact. Dylan pushed back in his chair almost as if he had been punched. "Bob Marley's music isn't political," Dylan told me. "Bob Marley's music is *universal*."

Bob Marley is still above the ground. To paraphrase Charles Dickens—Marley isn't dead: to begin with. "Because he put his all—his heart and soul and his life into his music, this is why it has the opportunity and the authority to live after him," Rita Marley, his widow, once told me. "There's no death to certain things. Just as there is a world without end, there are people with-out end." A few weeks before finishing my book, I took Dylan, my three-year-old son, to a picnic party. It was thrown by the com-pany where my wife, Sharon, works. Marley's music was booming from a small dance tent that had been set up. Songs about revolu-tion and Africa and slave drivers floated across grassy New Jersey fields. My son's eyes opened wide and he went running toward the tent, looking for Marley, eager to finally see in person the performer he so often listened to at home. I found the whole scene amusing, contradictory, and a little sad. Here was my son, searching in vain for a performer he loved but who had passed on a quarter century ago.

In many ways, I am just like my son. I have been running around, wide-eyed, looking for Bob Marley. I searched for him in libraries and record stores, in museums and recording studios, in mansions and tin-roofed shacks. After all, Marley told *Melody Maker* in 1979, "Death does not exist for me. I truly know God. He gives me this [life] and my estimation is: if he gives me this, why should he take it back? Only the Devil says everybody has to die." If you talk to my three-year-old, he'll tell you he's seen Bob Marley—behind a tree, in a passing car, walking down the street in broad daylight.

I think I've found him, too.

Let me introduce you to him.

STOP THAT TRAIN

You are in a small village in Jamaica during a misty morning on February 6, 1945, witnessing the birth of a baby. The community is Nine Miles, an area no bigger than a Brooklyn block, a place so tiny that it is named for its distance from the closest town of any significance, Alexandria. The mother, a black Jamaican woman named Cedella—most people called her Ciddy—is a teenager. Her labor cramps began two days ago as she attended daytime church services at Shiloh Apostolic Church. The father, an itinerant man named Norval St. Claire Marley—most people call him Captain—is in his sixties. He is Jamaican, but he likes to say that he is English. He was assumed to be white, but you will find that may not be entirely true. He first spotted Ciddy several years before. He may have met her on a train on its way to Montego Bay and followed her back to Nine Miles.

Ciddy remembers Norval as an impressive man who would parade around on a tall white horse. He may have grown in her memory. Norval was actually slightly built. He was five feet five and a half inches tall and weighed 124 pounds. He was secretive about his comings and goings and never owned a car. Most of his clothes were old and he didn't like to shave. Ciddy has said she was a virgin before she met Captain, and she became pregnant before they were married. Their marriage register, filed with the parish of St. Ann, is riddled with inaccuracies. The misinformation on the document may be a testament to the hasty and scandalous nature of their union. It was a marriage of black and white in a country where people were conscious of slight gradations of skin shades. The ceremony took place June 9, 1944. Cedella is listed on the register as "twenty" when she was actually eighteen years old. Norval is listed as "fifty" when he was sixty-three years old. Even his bride didn't know his real age—she thought he was ten years younger. He gives his father's name as "Robert Marley"—which was a common first name in the Marley clan. She correctly submits her father's name as "Omeriah Malcolm." Under "calling," she lists herself as a "domestic"—an accurate enough description. He calls himself a "clerk"—despite his having told folks throughout Nine Miles that he was in charge of parceling out British crown lands to war veterans and pensioners. A relative who knew him doubts that Norval, who was always borrowing money and never lasted long on any job, ever held such an important position. At best, he may have been serving as a surveyor's assistant. Ciddy would bear the Captain only one child before they separated forever. The newborn was seven pounds four ounces, and the afterbirth was taken and buried beneath the foot of a coconut tree. It would afterward be known as the baby's "friend tree." Captain, returning from a trip a few days after the delivery, gave his nameless offspring a name: Nesta Robert Marley.

Holding his new son in his arms, Captain said the baby's middle name, Robert, was a tribute to his older brother. Robert Marley, a well-known cricket and tennis player in his youth, had died at the age of sixty in May 1938. The *Jamaica Gleaner* had carried a lengthy obituary. It was evidence of the elevated status of the family in Jamaican social circles. Captain didn't tell his young bride what the unusual first name, Nesta, meant. Ciddy wasn't happy with the choice.

"Nesta?" said Ciddy. "I don't like dat name. People goin' call him 'Lester.' I know plenty man name Lester."

"Not Lester," said Captain. *"N-e-s-t-a."*

Ciddy would say later that she learned that the name meant "messenger."

Bob Marley's bestselling album, the greatest-hits collection *Legend*, was well named. The title evokes the mythic mist that has settled around his early life and times, obscuring facts and blurring his biography. A legend is more powerful than a lie. Lies can be proven untrue. A legend does not claim to be the whole truth, but it denies that it is entirely fallacious. It rests partly inside of history and partly outside. Legends, unlike lies, have a classical sheen. You feel good about passing legends along to your friends and down to your children. You feel guilty about lies. The Marley family history has been so tangled up in legends and lies, not even elders in the clan can always tell one from the other.

Nine Miles is located in the parish of St. Ann in Jamaica, a region that is traditionally called "the Garden Parish." Nobody knows exactly why the region has that particular designation. The island of Jamaica was formed about 150 million years ago when a series of underwater volcanoes rose above the waves. About 50 million years ago, the landmass sank back beneath the sea and was coated with decaying underwater life that hardened into limestone. Twenty million years ago, the area rose once more to become a flowering island in the middle of the Caribbean Sea. Fruits such as guava, pineapple, the prickly soursop, and the star apple have flourished on the island for hundreds of years. There are many mountains in Jamaica—nearly half the island is over three hundred meters (one thousand feet) above sea level. There are many rivers as well, and most of them are not navigable—they run down from the tall mountains into deep beds and their courses are interrupted by powerful waterfalls. Nearly three thousand varieties of flowering plants have been identified on the island, including eight hundred species found only in Jamaica. The Garden Parish is not unique for its abundance of vegetation—the whole island is a garden. Some say the name comes from a debate in the Jamaica House of Assembly in 1827, when the Honorable Lieutenant Colonel Hamilton Brown referred to his home area, fondly, as the garden parish. According to another story, there once was a charming lady who ran a tavern in the region who used to give guests the gift of a rose, plucked fresh from her garden.

Names are fluid things in Jamaica—from Cedella to Ciddy, Norval to Captain, Nesta to Robert to Bob—people and places often have multiple identities. Jamaican place-names are often whimsically descriptive. Wait-a-Bit, Trelawny, was named after the wait-a-bit thorn, which is said to have been used to form a hedge that blocked wild animals in Africa. Corn Puss Gap, St. Thomas, was named after a group of hikers that became stranded, caught a cat, "corned" it, and ate it. There are some names that were given by the Indians—the Tainos and then the Arawaks—tribes of farmers and fishermen who came from South America between AD 600 and AD 700 and were the first settlers of the island that would later be known as Jamaica. Guanaboa Vale, St. Catherine, is said to come from the Arawak word for soursop: *guanaba*. Sometimes appellations date back to the Spanish, who came to the island searching for gold. Christopher Columbus was the first European to land on Jamaica, and when he arrived at what is now known as St. Ann's Bay, he named it Santa Gloria "on account of the extreme beauty of its country." Columbus found the Indians with whom he traded to be exceedingly fair in their dealings—"We lost not the value of a pin," his son said about their exchanges. The Spanish were not as generous in their affairs. Spanish rule was chaotic, unproductive, and vicious. Hungry for gold, and bitterly disappointed that there was none to be found on the island, they exterminated nearly all the indigenous Indian inhabitants, reducing their population from approximately sixty thousand in 1509 to around sixty in 1655. The Jamaican historian Carey Robinson wrote this about conditions under the Spanish: "The island was badly defended, poverty stricken, underdeveloped, and underpopulated; the Government officials were indolent and demoralized, money was scarce and trade was falling off." In 1655, after decades of Spanish mismanagement, the British invaded the island with thirty-eight ships and eight thousand soldiers, and many names changed again. Caguaya, where the British landed, became Passage Fort. St. Jago de la Vega, the Spaniards' capital city, became simply Spanish Town.

In the Jamaica of Bob Marley's childhood, people who lived and loved across the color line were seen as tragic figures. They were trying, in vain, to move the immovable. Race was what kept society in order. Race was what kept the British on top and Africans on the bottom. People who crossed skin boundaries had to be rebuked. They were outcasts and outsiders. They were Oedipus wandering without sight or a kingdom. They were Norval and Nesta.

Norval had spent much of his life on the move. He was born in Jamaica in March 1881 to Robert Marley, a businessman of British stock who worked as an attorney for a property owner, and Ellen Bloomfield, a Jamaican woman who had roots in the parish of St. Ann, where her family owned a small coffee farm called Aboukir. Captain's older brother, also named Robert, was born in 1878. The boy's grand-uncle, Francis Marley, was identified as a member of the British Parliament in a *Gleaner* article in 1929. (According to the House of Commons Information Office, however, there is no record of a member of Parliament of that name around that time period.)

The Marley family has long presented itself to the world as white, but a wedding certificate for the marriage of Robert Marley and Ellen Bloomfield (who was eighteen years old at the time) lists him as "white" and her as "colored." Later generations of the Marley family were unaware of Bloomfield's racial designation. She may have passed for white. Bob Marley would face grief all his life for being the offspring of black and white. He would be teased, he would be ostracized, and he would question himself and his identity. The truth was, the "white" side of his family was racially mixed all along.

English colonialism is tangled up in race, but race is actually a fairly modern concept. The ancient Greeks didn't divide people according to physical characteristics. Anyone who wasn't Greek was a barbarian—but that could be solved by adopting Greek culture. The English language wouldn't include the word *race* until 1508, when it was used in a poem by William Dunbar. But by the time the English colonized Jamaica in the seventeenth century, race was one of the tools they employed to pacify the regions they conquered. The English were white. African slaves and their descendants were black. Race was fate. No matter that the ancient Greeks, who invented the Fates, did not believe in race.

Robert Marley apparently died before his children were adults. Young Norval and his brother were raised by their mother's family in Jamaica. Soon, like his grandfather, Norval developed wanderlust. He left Jamaica and worked for J. W. Flymers, in Niepe

Bay, Cuba, as a "ferro cement engineer," then turned up in England to join the British army in World War I. He signed up for duty in Liverpool on August 14, 1916, giving his last address as 31 Lord Nelson Street in Liverpool. He listed his place of birth as Croboro, Sussex (probably untrue—he may have expected better treatment in the army if he said he was native-born) and gave his physical condition as good. His health would soon deteriorate. During the war, he did not serve actively in Europe and was stationed at Prees Heath and Oswestry in Shropshire, England, near the border of Wales. His honorific of "Captain" was probably not a result of his army service—his army papers show that he was discharged as a private. After the army, Norval found work in Lagos, Nigeria, as a police officer—he may have picked up his title "Captain" while working for the military police there—and then visited South Africa as a member of the merchant navy.

Ciddy remembers Norval as an emotional man, given to weepy fits. He would sometimes sing "stones for my pillow/and the sky is my roof" and then burst into tears. His nephews would later say that they thought he suffered from "shell shock"—a condition associated with the survivors of trench warfare in World War I—while others speculated that he had become infected by a tsetse fly in Africa. Army records show that Norval applied for medical disability pension, stating that he suffered from "incontinence and a urinary stricture, and also rheumatism," and that these ailments were caused by "exposure" during his service with the army. The doctors who examined him stated in their reports that they could find no evidence of incontinence, but said that there "was evidence of an old stricture, the aggravation of which, if any, [by serving in the army] is presumed to have passed away." The doctors concluded that Norval suffered from "neurasthenia"—"a psychological disorder characterized by chronic fatigue and weakness, loss of memory, and generalized aches and pains, formerly thought to result from exhaustion of the nervous system." In other words, Norval had a nervous breakdown. (The term *neurasthenia* is no longer in scientific use.) Another medical-board report described Norval as "a neurotic type of man with no definite nerve symptoms" and found that there was "some creaking in [his] shoulders and knee joints." In May 1921, Norval was granted an interim 20 percent disability payment of eight shillings a week.

There is a story told about Norval Marley—on his side of the family—that on one occasion, his brother, Robert, and others were playing tennis at their Sandhurst estate in Kingston when Norval appeared at the wrought-iron gate. It was the first time anyone had seen him since he had disappeared years before. Spotting him, Robert paused in midserve, said, "He's returned," and continued playing. Another family story goes like this: Norval's mother was having a dinner party when she ran out of butter. It was the 1930s and Norval, who tended to live off the largesse of relatives, had been staying in her house. She asked Norval to take his horse and ride down to the corner store to get some more. About an hour later, the horse returned without a rider. His family didn't hear from Norval again until six months later when they received a postcard saying he had met a friend who offered him a job on a ship and that he was now in South Africa.

Chris Marley, a relative of Bob's on Norval's side of the family, said that in 1947, when he was six years old, he was staying with relatives at a house on Hillcrest Avenue in Kingston when a white man opened the street gate and walked around to the rear of the house.

"Who is that?" Chris asked.

He was shushed and told "never you mind." Years later, he learned that the white man was Uncle Norval, who had fallen on hard times and was being supported by his sister-in-law. Another relative remembers seeing Norval near the end of his life when he was ill. He was staying in a nursing home off of Half-Way Tree Road between Kingston and St. Andrew. While he was in the home, he was visited by three women—all of whom claimed to be married to him. Two of the women identified themselves as "Mrs. Marley." One of those women, perhaps, was Ciddy. She later sued Captain for bigamy but did not divorce him. Norval was defended on the charge by his nephew Cecil Marley, a lawyer, who successfully pleaded that he was senile. Said Ciddy: "There was no divorce. The church I was in didn't believe in it. But he got married to someone else. He was senile and died when Bob was around twelve years old." Ciddy would take Nesta to see Norval one last time. At the end of the visit, Norval gave his son a large copper one-cent coin known as a "Willie penny." Then he apologized, saying it was all he had to give him. Norval's journey had come to an end.

Nesta grew up in a one-room stone hut on a hill, sleeping in a single bed. Most of the dwellings in Nine Miles at that time would have been "wattle-and-daub" houses, built with sticks, covered with interwoven reeds, clay, and perhaps some cement, and whitened with lime. The roofs were made of palm fronds (families with a little more money used zinc sheets) and the floors were usually dirt. Captain had left soon after Nesta was born, explaining that because of a hernia, he could no longer ride a horse and so he was taking a position as a construction foreman for a bridge-building firm in Kingston. He had sent his family a few pounds on occasion, but the money soon trickled off. Nesta and his young mother were forced to fend mostly for themselves. Their house had a pile of stones outside that served as a stove, and there was an outhouse in the back. Nesta got up early, and he went to bed early. He loved the land and he loved to roam the forests around where he lived. There was a large solitary gray rock on which

Nesta would lay his head and look up at the sky. The house was surrounded on all sides by fruit trees—mango, jackfruit, naseberry, star apple, banana, coconut, ackee, avocado pear, and many citrus-bearing trees as well—orange, grapefruit, lime, and citron. There was no electricity in Nine Miles, and no running water. When the rains came, Nesta would walk down the hill to catch water. Sometimes he would pick a flower to bring back to his mother.

When he was still a child, he began to work the fields with his grandfather, Ciddy's father, Omeriah Malcolm. Some people called him Custos, a term of respect in Jamaica. Others called him Mass Amy—short for Master Omeriah. Still others called him Ma Name. He was not a churchgoing man, though he would read his Bible on occasion. He was a stern man, but he was a ladies' man as well, fathering some twenty to thirty children by a dozen or so women in the district. Although he was not rich, he was comfortable, and he owned his own house, the house that Ciddy and Nesta lived in, the surrounding lands, and a thirty-acre spread called Smith on a nearby mountaintop.

Work would begin before the sun came up. Nesta and one or more of his young relatives—Cousin Sledger, or Cousin Lloyd—would wake up at five o'clock in the morning, when it was still dark. He would boil some fish tea over the fire on the stone stove outside the house and drink it, and then walk through the hills to the property at Smith. Nesta would ride one of his grandfather's animals—Nimble the donkey, or a big gray horse.

"Where is my daddy today?" Nesta would sometimes ask Omeriah.

"Oh, your father is wearing his tall boots somewhere," Omeriah would reply.

The work was long, hard, and hot. Because Nesta was light-skinned, Omeriah often worried that he would burn in the sun, and sometimes tried to send him home early, but Nesta insisted on laboring as long as everyone else. To prepare the yam field, they would clear the ground, dig holes, and mash up the earth with manure. The cuttings from old yams were stuck in the holes, and peas were planted all around to attract snails and prevent them from attacking the yams. When the vines started, Nesta would stick poles in the dirt for them to run up. There were other crops to plant and harvest as well—cocoa bean, dasheen, corn, and sugarcane. At the end of the long day, if Nesta was riding the horse, he would race off down the hills. Omeriah had a gate in front of his house and Nesta would ride toward it at full speed, pull up, and have his horse leap into the air over the barrier. Says Sledger: "When Bob on the horse alone him dug inna the horse back like a tick! And the gate is about five feet tall."

Sundays were days of rest, and days of music. Ciddy was a member of the church choir, and Nesta joined, too. Said Bob, many years later: "We used to go to church and hear plenty singing, and watch people get in the spirit and all of that. That's what singing is, you know. Singing is a spirit. A spirit that don't talk, it sing . . . Me love harmony. From long time me hear plenty harmonies, even certain times some imaginary harmonies." Omeriah could play music, but preferred to hear songs outside of church. He had an organ, fiddle, and banjo, and sometimes he would play rumba music and get people dancing. Omeriah also owned a Delco generator, one of the only ones in the area, and on Sundays he would start it up and friends and family would gather round to listen to the radio. Sometimes they would hear a sermon, sometimes music from Cuba, sometimes tunes from America. Nesta often stopped by to listen. "I preferred dancing music," said Bob. "I listened to Ricky Nelson, Elvis, Fats Domino . . . that kind of thing was popular with Jamaican kids in the fifties. The only English-speaking radio station we heard was from Miami, but we got a lot of Latin stations, mostly from Cuba, before and after Castro."

Bob Marley once said, "My music fight against the system. My music defend righteousness." Using music as a weapon was part of his family history. On his mother's side, the family had a blood link to a group of Jamaican freedom fighters called the Maroons. After the British invasion, the black inhabitants of the island— many of them slaves from the Gold Coast of Africa who first arrived around 1517—fled to the hills and forests of Jamaica. There, they founded their own towns and came up with their own names for the people and places on the island, using a language that was a mix of words from their native lands and words they'd picked up from the Spanish and their English successors. The British and Spanish had plenty of names for the black rebels. They were called "wild Negroes," "fugitive Negroes," and "Rebellious Negroes." The Spanish called escaped domestic animals, like cows and horses, *cimarrones;* perhaps, in a derivation from that word, the blacks who escaped to live in the untamed interior regions of Jamaica were soon called by a new name: Maroons.

Music was an important part of the Maroon arsenal. British soldiers, over hundreds of years of fighting, were almost never able to successfully surprise Maroon troops. On March 12, 1656, Major General Sedgwicke of the British forces wrote back to his superiors in England about the Maroon threat: "Concerning the state of the enemy on shore here, the Spaniard is not considerable, but of the Blacks there are many, who are like to prove as thorns and pricks in our sides, living in the mountains and woods, a kind of life both natural and I believe acceptable to them. There scarce a week passeth without one or two slain by them, and as we grow secure, they grow bold and bloody." Maroon lookouts were armed with an abeng, which is a cow horn with a hole at the tip and a blowhole on one side. *Abeng* is an Akan word meaning "horn." Whenever a Maroon lookout spotted trouble, he would blow on his abeng. A wide and complex variety of calls were employed, and it was said that a skilled abeng player could refer to an individual Maroon soldier by name simply by blowing his horn. The British, despite their superior numbers and supposedly advanced weaponry, had no way of signaling to one another over long distances. Using the abeng to rally their forces, Maroons staged many surprise attacks against them.

In Jamaica, the ethnic group that made up the bulk of the Maroons is known as the Koromantee or the Coromantie. There is no such corresponding tribe in Africa; it's a loose term that came to refer to the Ashanti, Akan, Twi, and Fanti peoples, all of whom had been brought to an area known as Koromantee in Ghana before being shipped off as slaves to the New World. The Koromantees, once they reached the New World, developed a reputation for bravery, resourcefulness, and rebelliousness. They led many of the rebellions that took place in Jamaica between 1655 and the 1830s, which eventually helped force the English to free their slaves.

Sir Hans Sloane, who founded the British Museum, wrote this about the way discipline was maintained on Jamaican estates: for negligence, slaves were "whipped by the overseer with lancewood switches till they be bloody, and several of the switches broken . . . after they are whipped till they are raw, some put on their skin pepper and salt to make them smart; at other times their masters will drop melted wax on their skins, and use several very exquisite tortures." Running away would result in this punishment: "Iron wings of great weight upon their ankles, or pothooks about their necks, which are iron rings with two long rods riveted to them, or a spur in the mouth [a gag]." Insurrection was a capital offense resulting in the perpetrator being burned alive: "He was fastened down on the ground with crooked sticks on every limb; they then applied the fire by degrees, from the feet and hands, burning them gradually up the head, whereby the pains are extravagant." Sloane concluded his report: "These punishments are sometimes merited by the blacks, who are a very perverse generation of people; and though they appear harsh, yet are scarce equal to some of their crimes."

The Maroons fought a successful guerrilla war against the British—then the most powerful empire in human history—for almost two centuries. Led by the military genius of Maroon warriors like Cudjoe and his brothers, Accompong and Johnny, they were outgunned and outmanned, but relied on techniques suited to their environment to outmaneuver their foes. In 1764, Maroon fighters gave a peaceful demonstration of their gymnastic fighting style to the governor of Jamaica. Historian Edward Long, in his three-volume *History of Jamaica* published in 1774, captured the scene: "With amazing ability they ran, or rather rolled, through various firings and evolutions. This part of their exercise indeed more justly deserves to be [styled] evolution than any that is practiced by regular troops, for they fire stooping almost to the very ground, and no sooner are their muskets discharged than they throw themselves into a thousand antic gestures, and tumble over and over, so as to be continually shifting their place; the intention of which is to elude the shot as well as to deceive the aim of their adversaries which their nimble and almost instantaneous change of position renders extremely uncertain."

There was a mystic nature to the Maroon fighting style that the British were never fully able to appreciate or overcome. In 1738, exhausted from decades of fighting, the British forces commissioned a Colonel Guthrie to seek out the Maroon leader Cudjoe and sue for peace. Cudjoe traveled down the winding mountain paths to meet with his longtime enemies at Petty River Bottom. He was around sixty years old at the time, and had been fighting since he was about twelve. The day he met Colonel Guthrie,

Cudjoe was wearing a tattered old blue coat, white knee pants, a head tie, and a small round hat. He carried with him a long musket, a bag of shot, a powder horn, and a machete in a leather sheath he had tucked under his armpit. The treaty was agreed to on March 1, 1739, and signed underneath a large cotton tree, which was afterward known as "Cudjoe's Tree." The Maroons were guaranteed autonomy in their lands, and Cudjoe's brothers, Accompong and Johnny, were named his successors. After the signing, Cudjoe trekked back to his home in the mountains.

Around the age of four, Nesta began to read palms. Ciddy would hear stories about his fortune-telling from friends, relatives, and neighbors. She put little stock in it; Nesta was only a small boy, after all, and people were always telling stories of weird goings-on in the Jamaican countryside—stories of duppies (a kind of Jamaican ghost), of rolling calves (cows that burn with mysterious fire), and the like. Nanny, a Maroon warrior queen, was said to have possessed the ability to catch bullets in the air. One day, a relative, Aunt Zen, came to Ciddy to tell her another tale.

"You know, Auntie Ciddy, Nesta can really read hands," said Aunt Zen.

"He's just playing," replied Ciddy.

But Ciddy knew that there was a mystic streak in her family. Omeriah's father was descended from the Koromantee people, specifically the Ashanti tribe. Through Maroon culture, many aspects of African culture were preserved—including supernatural practices and rituals. Omeriah was known around the area as a skilled myalman. Myalmen were direct descendants of African medicine men. Practitioners were part of a secret society that preserved the use of herbs and dances to cure the sick. The British tried to stamp out myalism in Jamaica in 1843 through prosecutions and by dispatching a large number of special constables to various parishes. The practice refused to die. Myalmen were often seen as the counter to obeahmen. Obeahmen were "shadow takers," who were thought to steal people's spirits and thus bring on illness or death. Myalmen, the "shadow catchers," would use their "science" to recapture souls and restore the spirits of the infirm. While the obeahman often conducted his rituals in a graveyard, the myalman conducted his ceremonies around a cotton tree, which was thought to be the locus of power for the spirit world. Dancing was another important part of the myalist creed. In 1818, Monk Lewis witnessed a ritual in which myalmen danced until they seemingly fell dead from exhaustion and then were revived when the juice from various herbs was squeezed into their mouths. A myalman was often called a "four-eyed man" because he had the power to see where a soul was being imprisoned. He could help free such souls with his dance. When Nesta was an ailing six-month-old infant, Omeriah used his skills as a myalman to nurse him back to health. Said Omeriah: "Evil spirits play wid de baby."

At age four, Nesta began attending the nearby Stepney School. He was a bright child and often tutored the other students in counting and reading. But Nesta soon came to take more interest in singing than in his other lessons.

· "Who can write, write," his teacher told him. "Who can sing, sing."

Nesta decided to sing. At lunchtime at school, he would play soccer—with oranges or grapefruits used instead of a ball—and when all the running and kicking was done, he would sing—so softly that he could barely be heard. Despite his soft voice, he won a pound at a local singing contest held at Fig Tree Corner. When Nesta was six, Captain wrote Ciddy and asked that the child be sent to Kingston for tutoring. Captain came for the child and took him into Kingston. It was one of the only times Nesta would ever see his father. The reunion didn't last long. Captain dropped Nesta off at the home of a white woman named Mrs. Grey. For a year, Ciddy heard no word and didn't know Nesta's whereabouts. A family friend, Maggy James, spotted Nesta walking on Spanish Town Road in the city and told Ciddy about it. Ciddy traveled to Kingston herself and took her boy home.

There has never been extensive train service in Jamaica. The mountains, forests, and rivers make the construction of railways a difficult and expensive proposition. The most frequently boarded trains are rails of the imagination. Train imagery, however, is common in Jamaican song, a metaphorical import from England and from the blues, soul, and country songs islanders have heard on American radio programs. So trains come and go, in songs like "Midnight Track" by Owen Gray, and "Train to Skaville" by the Ethiopians, and "Down by the Train Line" by the Spanishtonians, which was later recorded as "Draw Your Brakes" by Scotty for the soundtrack to the 1972 reggae movie *The Harder They Come*. The Wailers' first album for Island Records, *Catch a Fire*, would feature a song titled "Stop That Train."

Trains, for Jamaicans, became symbols of escape, even if there were not that many real trains to catch. There are many Jamaicans who are always hoping to go somewhere, even if they are going nowhere. Some folks living in the country want to go to the city; some residents of the city dream of returning to the country. Still others have visions of leaving for America, and more than a few Jamaicans who have left for America long to return home. And so the fantasy train travels on, making impossible journeys.

St. Ann has never had passenger rail service, but when Nesta was growing up, there was a popular children's song called "Linstead Train a Come" about trains in a neighboring parish. At the time, people living in that area would sometimes travel to Kingston by hopping on a mail coach that had connections at Linstead and Ewarton. When kids sang the song, they would form a line with friends and shuffle forward or backward in accordance to the lyrics.

Linstead train a come, pah, pah
Everybody come together
Ewarton train a come, pah, pah
Everybody back together, pah, pah

The song of the city was calling out to Nesta. One of his best friends was Neville O'Riley Livingston, nicknamed Bunny. He was a slight, energetic child who was serious about his schoolwork. He was equally serious about his pastimes. When Bunny did something, he applied himself. He had no time for foolishness. The two had met when Nesta was eleven years old and Bunny was nine. They attended the Stepney School in St. Ann together. Bunny had moved to Kingston and then moved back to Nine Miles when he was around ten years old. He had brought with him something that fascinated Nesta: a homemade guitar, crafted out of a bamboo stick, electrical wire, and a sardine can. "In Kingston, in the city, kids are inclined to always be making their own little devices, your own little trucks, your own little skates, your own little stuff like that," explains Bunny. "So I was accustomed to making my own guitar, as music was something that was instilled in me, it was born inside of me. So when I went to the country I would introduce that to the country youth as one of my things—one of my city hobbies."

As kids left school, or parents returned from work, Bunny would sit outside playing his guitar and singing songs that he had learned. He would perform tunes by Rosco Gordon and Louis Jordan. He would sing "Seven Lonely Days" and "Sentimental Journey." They were numbers he had heard on the radio in Kingston. It was the kind of music folks in Nine Miles were not accustomed to hearing regularly on the radio, because of the limited reception. Bunny was happy to introduce them to a new world of sound: "You had to make your own noise, you had to make your own entertainment." Nesta was entranced by what he heard. He decided to take up the guitar—and the instrument became intimately linked to his songwriting. He said later: "Well, it grow together. Is like, first time mi try to write a song is the first time mi try to play the guitar. And soh mi can write a song without the guitar. But it really grow together. Mi really like stay with mi guitar. But it just happen, is Jah inspiration come thru man."

Ciddy could see that her son had dreams beyond Nine Miles. She wanted better things for him. But she didn't want to be separated from him again. She soon came to realize that Nesta could take care of himself.

On occasion, she would confront Nesta when he disappeared without explanation.

"Where were you?" Ciddy asked.

"With my friends," Nesta answered.

"Suppose they make you do something wrong?"

"Mama, no one can make me do wrong," said Nesta. "When there is a quarrel, you don't just quarrel back, just take it easy."

Ciddy decided to keep quiet and leave her child to his own devices.

She left Nine Miles to find work. Ciddy first tried "higgling" in Kingston—selling food at a city market. But the trip down to Kingston from Nine Miles was long and wearing—she hitched a ride on the back of a truck to save money—and she was ripped off by market thieves who distracted her and stole her goods. After that, she found a job as a live-in maid in St. Andrew. She would cook and clean in exchange for a small salary plus room and board. She saved what she could and sent it back to Nesta in the country. She missed her child and searched for a way for them to be together.

A relative came through. Ciddy's Aunt Ivy invited her to come to Kingston and share an apartment on Beckford Street. Aunt Ivy lived alone in the apartment with her daughter and was having trouble making the rent. If Ciddy and Nesta were to move in, their help would be welcome. There was a complication, however. Not long before this, Ciddy and Bunny's father, Thaddius "Toddy" Livingston, had begun a relationship in the hills of Nine Miles. They eventually had a daughter together. Bunny and his father were also planning to move from Nine Miles to Kingston. Recalls Bunny: "We were like brothers before we were in the Wailers, because we shared the same sister. We grew up as family, we became family, that's before any song was sung." So two weeks after the offer from Aunt Ivy, Nesta took a bus into Kingston to meet his mother, and to link up with his new extended family. Ciddy, Nesta, and Bunny and his father soon moved in together in Kingston. Nesta, like Cudjoe before him, was now ready to take on the world with his brothers in arms.

CONCRETE JUNGLE

Bob Marley believed that music had no color. Nonetheless, executives in the music industry have long assigned their product a race. In fact, in the early part of the twentieth century, the music business had a name for the kind of songs that blacks performed: race music. From the birth of the blues in America, the music industry has practiced a kind of entertainment apartheid. The soul music that Marley longed to hear growing up was shunned by Jamaican radio. He had to search out stray American signals to hear its echoes. Walk into a music store today, you will often find recordings by white artists clustered in one part of the store, and works by black artists in another. In music, segregation is expected and accepted. It has long been commonly assumed that whites and blacks make different kinds of music and listen to different kinds of music because they lead different kinds of lives. The reality was different. The exotic became erotic. Separation sparked desire. White fans constantly crossed the color line to listen to the music they were forbidden to listen to. Some white artists crossed the color line to make the music they were supposed to be unable to make.

Virtually every major genre of pop music born in the twentieth century—including blues, rock, and rap—has its roots in the black experience. In almost every case, the commercial superstar that emerged to represent the genre has been white. The white British blues guitarist Eric Clapton has sold more records than any other black blues musician. "Clapton is God" graffiti was seen scrawled around London in the 1960s. There was no graffiti proclaiming the divinity of Son House or Memphis Minnie. Elvis has been hailed by many as the inventor of rock and roll, despite the fact that his first big hit, "That's All Right Mama," was a reworking of a song by a black musician, Arthur "Big Boy" Crudup, and that Ike Turner was performing rock years before Presley, and that Presley used to study Turner and Crudup to hone his act. The white hip-hop trio Beastie Boys scored the first rap album to sell a million copies and Eminem became the first rap artist to win an Oscar for best song. Langston Hughes once famously moaned that they had "taken my blues and gone." They didn't go far. They came back to take rock and hip-hop, too.

There is, however, one major genre of pop music in which a black performer is widely considered, by both blacks and whites, to be its most iconic star. The music is reggae and the artist is Bob Marley. He managed to break through racial constraints in a way that his black counterparts in other genres were unable to do. Yes, one may argue that Michael Jackson was the King of Pop, but he lost his nose, his skin tone, and perhaps his soul in exchange for the coronation. Marley made no such concessions. Just as he challenged color barriers in life, he transcended them in his art.

His battle began in the trenches.

Nesta lived in various homes around Kingston. In the city, he had taken on a new name. Friends began to call him Robert, Robby, or Bob. Some even called him Lester, just as his mother had feared when his father had given him his odd name, Nesta. Bob and his mother wound up in Trench Town, a ghetto area, living with Toddy and Bunny. Kingston was an overwhelming city. Cars were jammed bumper to bumper. Dogs and hogs wandered freely on busy streets. Higglers shouted out their wares on the roadside. Squatters peeked out from the blown-out windows of abandoned buildings. Cows grazed along grassy strips by the roadside. Girls and boys in school uniforms laughed and congregated at the intersections. When the singer Toots Hibbert first journeyed from his country home in May Pen to Kingston around this same period, he said he "felt like I was in New York City. I had never been to New York, but I thought it couldn't feel any bigger." In many ways, Kingston was Jamaica. About 40 percent of the island's population lived in that one city. Bob had gone from milking goats to catching buses, from carrying rainwater to running water, from the green hills of Nine Miles to the concrete shacks of Trench Town.

Kingston was born in an earthquake. There was no such place as Kingston, Jamaica, before 1692. The area that is now called central Kingston had another name back then: Colonel Samuel Barry's Hog Crawle. It was an accurate description of how the land was then put to use. There were only eight or nine houses in the area, spread out around some 530 acres of the Liguanea Plain. But across the harbor, there was a real town: Port Royal. It was known, around the world, as the "wickedest city on earth." It was frequented by pirates such as Blackbeard (one eighteenth-century chronicler wrote of him: "imagination cannot form an idea of a

fury, from Hell, to look more frightful") and Anne Bonny and
Mary Read (two women who dressed as men and set sail as buc-
caneers). Much of this piracy was winked at, even supported, by
the local authorities. The pirate politician Henry Morgan carried
out raids with the approval of the Council of Jamaica. He later
served as lieutenant governor before dying of dropsy brought on
by the fact he was "much given to drinking and sitting up late."
Morgan's lawless conduct helped solidify the idea in the public
imagination that Jamaican government officials were little more
than pirates in disguise. Pirates would crop up in a number of
Wailers songs, including "You Can't Blame the Youth" and "Redemption Song."

Seventeenth-century writer Ned Ward in *A Trip to Jamaica:
With a True Character of the People and the Island* called Port
Royal "the dunghill of the universe, the refuse of the whole
creation, the clippings of the elements, a shapeless pile of rub-
bish confusd'ly jumbl'd into an emblem of the chaos, neglected
by Omnipotence when he form'd the world into its admirable
order . . . the very Sodom of the universe." Port Royal eventually met the same fate as Sodom: total destruction. On June
7,1692, the entire city was swallowed up in an earthquake, killing more than five thousand people. One report at the time
called the catastrophe "a dreadful warning to the sleepy world:
or God's judgements shewed on a sinful people, as a fore-
runner of the terrible day of the Lord." On July 22, 1692, the
Council of Jamaica passed regulations with regard to the construction of a "towne to be called Kingston." And so the new
city was born.

The Kingston-born novelist Marlon James says that the Jamaican countryside in which Bob Marley grew up in the 1950s was
not that much different from the Jamaican countryside of the

1850s. There was the same stern Christianity, alongside thriving belief in mysticism. There was the same unforgiving sexual prudishness, alongside rampant out-of-wedlock births. There was the same colonial mind-set, once enforced by British guns, now carried on in the successfully indoctrinated Jamaican hearts.

Jamaica is an island out of time. There is no spring, summer, fall, or winter. There is only the wet season and the dry season. It is only raining or not raining. Sometimes there are great winds and high waves. It is always warm. It is never cold. It is always green. The resistance to change is not limited to the natural world. The cars on the road are years out-of-date. The buildings on the streets are faded versions of themselves from happier times. The monuments celebrate heroes from a distant past and often from distant shores. Stories from hundreds of years ago are often told as if they occurred just yesterday. In the ancestral home of the seventeenth-century Maroon warrior woman Nanny, a glass of water is left for her every night and some residents speak of her as if she were still among the living.

Bob came to Kingston with few clothes and no money. He dressed as he had in the country because he wasn't able to afford city garb. Poverty creates a kind of time warp. When you have little money to spend, you put things off. Purchases are put off for another day. Decisions are put off for when things are better, whenever that day may be. Dreams are put off until fantasies can be financed. You sleep in the same bed, with its broken springs, because there is no money for another, not now. You wear the same clothes, because the shirt isn't that threadbare, not yet, and the shoes can last at least another few months. You slip into your own past, wear it on your back every day, because there is no money to buy a new future. Not now, maybe later.

Bob, in his early days in Trench Town, discovered that it was difficult to find the future because it was difficult to fund. The island, poverty, and the people around him were ceaselessly pulling him back into the past.

Initially, Bob had some trouble finding his way in Kingston. Part of his problem was that he was a country boy trying to make it in the city. Life in the country was slower and gentler than life in Jamaica's urban centers. Another part of his difficulty, perhaps the larger portion, came with being a mixed-race kid. Kingston is a jumble of races and cultures—there are black Jamaicans, white Jamaicans, Asian Jamaicans, and many multiracial Jamaicans. Though the motto of the country is "Out of Many One People," the slogan is misleading. The country isn't as diverse as its dreams. Ninety-one percent of the population is African or Afro-European; another 5 percent is mixed African, East Indian, Asian, or other descent; and only 0.8 percent is European. Jamaican officials like to think of the country as more varied than it is, in part because they like to imagine the nation as whiter than it is. Jamaica's motto could well have been "Out of Pretty Much a Single Race, a Sharply Divided People." But that wouldn't be quite as racially comforting. Barriers of class separate people in Jamaica and they are as ugly and ubiquitous as the corrugated tin fences that run through Trench Town. Asians, whites, and people of mixed-race backgrounds form a disproportionately large part of the ownership class. Jamaicans of primarily African heritage make up a disproportionately large part of the working class and unemployed. The racial and economic inequities have legal roots. The Consolidated Slave Laws of 1792 created an apartheid-like state that regulated where slaves could travel and their legal right to assemble. Jamaicans of mixed race were required to carry certificates of freedom. Slavery was abolished in Jamaica in 1834, but its legacy poisoned interaction between the races for decades afterward. Black self-hatred, nurtured by European control, wormed its way into such Jamaican folk sayings as "Every John Crow think him pickney white, and every jackass think him cubby racehorse pickney." Needless to say, that maxim was not in the running for Jamaica's national credo.

Friends of Bob, when he was a kid in Trench Town, say that he would often get into fights because he was lighter than most other slum residents. Packs of bullies would call him "the little red bwoy" or "the little yellow bwoy" and beat him up. Bob would not have appeared red, yellow, or mixed to many non-Jamaicans. In South Carolina at the time, he would have been just another brown-skinned Negro. But in Trench Town, a little lightness went a long way. Bob tried to fight back by not fighting, but when he tried to reach out, his red/yellow/brown-skinned hand was often slapped back. He took up with a black girlfriend, but her family ended the relationship because they didn't want "no white man in our breed." The rejection left Bob depressed and he threatened to kill himself.

"Why am I this person? Why is my father white and not black like everybody else? What did I do wrong?" Bob asked Cedella.

She had no answers.

There is a historical dispute over exactly how Trench Town got its name. Some say the name came from a large trench that ran through the squatter camps. Others say Mr. Trench was a builder on the project and became its namesake. It was developed as low-income housing in the 1920s. Its planners hoped that the area would provide comfortable and dignified housing for war veterans, but it was soon on the decline. Between 1921 and 1943, the population in the Kingston metro area doubled from 60,000 to 120,000. One city survey found an average density of 3.6 people per room. In Trench Town, it became not uncommon for 8 people to share a single room, and in 1951, the year of a devastating hurricane, the area was registered as one of four squatter camps in Kingston by the Central Housing Authority. As a result of its status, the name Trench Town may have had roots in a slight. In Jamaica, localities whose names end with "town," like Trench Town or Denham Town, are often located in poor areas with reduced city services.

The visiting English writer Patrick Leigh Fermor wrote in his book *The Traveller's Tree* (1950): "Trench Town is a labyrinth of slender alley-ways. Warm and sinuous troughs of dust uncoil between tall hedges of candelabra cactus. In the blaze of the moonshine it looks secret and mysterious and astonishingly beautiful. Gaps in the bristling palisades revealed huts of timber and palm-leaf and dusty courtyards: cool and silvery expanses with here and there a donkey or a couple of goats—portentous figures in that brilliant light—munching above the dark pools of their own shadows." It was a poetic, if overly romantic, rendering of the reality. Life in Trench Town was hard, and young Bob was one of the "sufferers." His cousin Sledger, who moved into the city around the same time as Bob, said the two would sometimes go weeks without a solid meal. But Bob wouldn't beg. He refused to ask anyone for help. He wanted to succeed on his own terms. He would often drink water in an effort to quench his hunger.

The residents of Trench Town embraced their neighborhood with a mix of defiance and pride. They knew they didn't have much, but they were able to find some measure of satisfaction in what they had. Transportation Bus No. 19 took people into the area. A reservoir on Thirteenth Street provided fresh water. A clinic on Eighth Street offered health-care services. Stores were usually well stocked with food, and prices were negotiable. To the north and south there were Calvary and May Pen cemeteries, respectively, to bury the dead.

And above all there was the sound of song. Music was the star attraction in Trench Town. Music echoed out of the many storefront churches. There was revival chanting, foot stomping, drumming, hand clapping—and not just on Sunday, but throughout the week, day and night. It is said that Jamaica has more churches per capita than any other country in the world. In Trench Town, for every church there seemed to be a dance hall—and they pumped out music to match the churches, at all hours, and not just on weekends. Ears and hearts and feet were pulled this way and that by music. Rhythms and lyrics and melodies were vying for attention and souls. Songs seeped into the skin and spirits of the residents.

Bob's Trench Town days were tough. But when the music hits, you feel no pain. Songs blasted from jukeboxes in bars, and from amateur musicians jamming with one another. Kingston attracted top performers. Bob saw Brook Benton come down to the city to do a show. He was thrilled when Dinah Washington paid a visit. In the countryside, music was hard to find. In the city, there seemed to be music in every alleyway. Every street seemed to have a theme song. Walking down Barrett Street in the late 1950s, Bob heard early rock hits, like LaVern Baker's "Jim Dandy to the Rescue" and Chuck Willis's "What Am I Living For?" On Oxford Street, he would listen to Nat King Cole and Billy Eckstine. On Regent Street, there were the sounds of calypso and steel drums as well as Fats Domino, Ricky Nelson, and Elvis Presley. Bob breathed it all in.

But it was in Trench Town where the beat was the strongest. People in Trench Town came to believe that if you lived there, you knew more about music than if you lived elsewhere on the island, and that you were more adept at performing it. Trench Town was viewed by its citizens as the Motown of Jamaica. A number of the area's residents went on to become singing stars, including Higgs & Wilson, Alton and Eddy, the School Boys, Delroy Wilson, Hortense Ellis, and Jimmy Tucker.

Bob would draw heavily on his lean years in his later work. It is often only the rich who have the time to sing about being poor. When artists who lack a deep understanding of hardship try to address the subject, the penniless and the homeless can be turned into faceless art. They can become symbols without substance, creatures to be pitied and helped. They are to be shown sympathy, but perhaps not empathy. The songs are about them but not for them. Bob lived among the suffering and suffered along with them. There was no separation between the singer and his song. Because he wrote many of his lyrics while he was struggling to make a living, his songs are full of life. His work has all the details of life on the margins because of his firsthand observation, firsthand touch, taste, smell, and hearing. He would sing of "Trench Town Rock," of sharing the shelter of a single bed, and the light of a communal fire. He would condemn the "Rat Race" and the "Babylon System" because he had struggled through oppressive restrictions. He had seen friends get arrested. He had lived without a home. He had gone without a job. He would sing of these things and more because he had experienced them.

But poverty is romantic only in retrospect. Those years created something hard in Bob. He began to smile less and scowl more. He focused his efforts and didn't like to waste time. He was generous with his money, once he got some, but he was intolerant of those who squandered what they had. He celebrated freedom in his music, but cherished organization in his life. He liked to keep his living spaces clean, with everything in its right place. He took frequent baths and washed his hair every day. He grew more observant of the people, events, and things around him, always looking for opportunities that he could use to propel himself out of his circumstances. He turned to structure to save himself from despair and dissolution. If everything could be just so, then everything would be all right. He didn't so much want to escape Trench Town as he wanted to have the ability to leave Trench Town. He wanted a choice. Even when he eventually moved, he never left. He approached songwriting, and life, with the eyes of a man who had eaten too many dinners of cornmeal porridge.

Bob would return to Trench Town in his songwriting because he couldn't leave. The effort it took to get out would mark him forever. It would always make him one of the people even when he was considered one of the gods. He was able to employ the same clear-eyed vision he used to find a path out of poverty to look back and create songs that evoked his early days without pity, without overstatement, and with an authority that was without peer. He had passed through the eye of the needle only to return. When he became a legend he would drive a BMW, but he would always leave the doors unlocked. He was one of the people. And why would the people steal something from their own?

When Bob and Bunny first arrived in Kingston, they had one priority: schoolbooks. Bob attended St. Aloysius Primary School, and Bunny attended All Saints' Primary School. Bunny would see his friend often, although they were going to classes at different institutions. Bunny was a kind of magic realist. He believed in the supernatural and that there was a deep enchantment that existed in the natural world. He felt a connection to trees, to water, to land, to animals. But he also believed in hard work. He trusted results that you could see. He was friendly with those who had earned his trust with deeds and not words. And he firmly believed that if you wanted to accomplish something, you had to be prepared to work hard at it and get your hands dirty. Despite the fact that Bob was new to the city, Bunny never felt he had to show his friend the ropes. Bob wasn't the kind of guy who had to be shown the ropes. He figured things out, and usually pretty fast.

Despite his scrapes with other Trench Town youths, Bob was no tattletale. From his first days in Kingston, he showed a strong devotion to his friends. Cedella would tell him, "You play too rough," "Don't go here," and "Don't go there." But she couldn't stop him from going around town with his new companions. Besides, she had work to do and money to earn. After Bob moved to Kingston, Cedella found employment at a restaurant on the corner of Charles Street and Spanish Town Road. One day a little boy came in.

"Are you Robert's mother?" asked the boy.

"Yes," Cedella replied. "What happen?" From the way he came in, she knew that something was wrong.

"He get a chop."

"He what?"

"He get a chop on his face."

"Where?"

"The school."

There was a school on Spanish Town Road behind the market. Cedella quickly closed up the restaurant and asked the man next door, who ran a shoe store, to keep an eye on things until she returned.

She soon spotted Bob with some friends—or at least she thought she did. Bob appeared to be wounded. He and his friends quickly ran out of sight and Cedella couldn't catch up to them.

Later, when Bob came home, he tried to hide his injury, but she could see that his face was hurt. Had Bob been in another fight about his skin color? He didn't say.

"Nesta, what you doing out there?" said Cedella.

"Nothing."

"What chop you?"

"The boys."

"Why did you run from me when I tried to call you?"

"Well, I thought you were going to call police on them, and is me good friend."

Bunny would comment later: "The only thing I can recall Trench Town not having was a police station . . . Above all, the people of Trench Town did not like informers. One could be whipped for doing that."

Bunny and Bob shared a love of sports. Bunny loved swimming, table tennis, boxing, cricket, and soccer. Bob loved running, cricket, and soccer. The two boys would always find time to kick a soccer ball around. Said Bob: "Yes I was playin' at school, y'know I never play for no big club or anything like that, just at school in Trench Town. Football is a part of I, keep you out of trouble. Discipline, y'know. Mek you run in the morningtime. When you run you clear out your head. The world wake up round you—you're going a long time, you know what I mean?"

Bob grew increasingly skeptical about what he was being taught at school. Said Bob: "Everyone who go to school, if you don't mind sharp, you learn in school 'bout Christopher Columbus, Marco Polo . . . What about the tradition of the African people? We want to learn that in school. We don't want to learn about Christopher Columbus and all of that. Because all it lead you to do is be a criminal. When you study how these people went to Jamaica, see the Arawak Indians living there and killed them off and then them say they discovered the land. That is just pure rape and murder and piracy."

Jamaicans have long had a love for learning—even if they had to leave their underfunded schools to get it. One official report from the Ministry of Education said of the primary schools: "The system is critically handicapped by irregularity of attendance, gross overcrowding, vestigial equipment and instructional materials and inadequate numbers of teachers, trained and untrained. Conditions are so primitive that the mind boggles at the thought of the conditions under which teachers must teach and children learn." Despite this, one estimate found that almost 90 percent of Jamaicans are literate.

Bob's attention started to turn away from school and games and toward the arts. He wrote poetry and published it in a local magazine. He thought more about songwriting. Music had been a hobby for Bunny. But Bob took it seriously. He saw it as a career, and a way out. As he attended classes and heard teachers droning on about Henry Morgan and other historical figures he cared little about, music drowned out their drones. He decided he wanted to be a singer, and that he wanted to do it full-time.

His mother didn't think singing was a viable career. When he came home late at night she would confront him. Where had he been? Who had he been with? She would often have something in her hands to beat him with. Bob would tell her he had been rehearsing. Cedella didn't understand. What was he rehearsing? Songs? That just didn't seem realistic to her. Bob needed to focus. He needed to do something practical.

Bob decided to follow his mother's advice and learn a trade. Cedella knew men who were welders and she told Bob that he should offer himself up as an apprentice. Bob hated the idea, but reported to work at the welding yard anyway. One day he was welding some steel and a piece of metal flew off and got stuck in the white of his eye. He had to go to the hospital to have it taken out.

Cedella was distraught when she saw the terrible pain her son was in. She was the one who had encouraged him to take the job. "Oh my God, it can't be like this!" she cried.

"You nuh hear me say is nothing else me want to do beside sing?" Bob responded.

Bob was finished with welding. "I loved to sing, so I thought I might as well take the chance," he said. "Welding was too hard!" Bob tracked down some of his "white" relatives in Kingston and asked them for money so he could start a music career. Some of them had no idea who he was and didn't believe they were related. He may have gotten some money, but he mostly received rejection. Lacking outside support, Bob turned within. Old men, he would say, have plans, but young men have visions. He envisioned himself making music and having great success. Bob was having trouble, however, turning his visions into reality. He tried out for a local producer, Leslie Kong, but was rejected without explanation.

When Bob was a teen and working as a welder, he had befriended another worker in the yard named Desmond Dekker. Dekker also wanted to be a professional singer. He had gone to a local record shop, Beverley's, and auditioned successfully. His song "Honour Your Father and Your Mother" was recorded for release. Triumphant, he came back to tell Bob about his good fortune.

"Bwoy, I meet up with two bredren who help me get my music recorded. Them 'ave put me on record," Dekker told Bob.

"Go 'way, yuh lie!" Bob said.

Dekker agreed to help Bob land a record contract of his own. He would introduce him to the scout for Beverley's who had signed him: a singer named Jimmy Cliff.

Jimmy Cliff was born James Chambers in Somerton, Jamaica, twelve miles outside of Montego Bay, on April 1, 1948. Like Marley, he was a descendant of the Maroons. His father was a tailor with only a small income, his mother was a domestic who left home when Cliff was still a child. Jimmy liked the idea of associating his name with heights and so he changed his stage name to Cliff. When he came to Kingston, he found it difficult to break into the music business. He was already poor, and money got tighter. He was so hungry, he thought about stealing to eat, but he couldn't stop thinking about how ashamed his father would be if his son became a petty thief. So he kept pushing to make it as a musician. In 1962, Cliff made his first record, "Daisy Got Me Crazy," for a Jamaican producer named Count Boysie. It was never widely released and Cliff said he was never paid for recording it—a common problem for Jamaican singers. At the time, Cliff didn't know anything about royalties. And asking about a contract was the quickest way to get fired. He was just happy to be in the studio, and more than willing to perform for whichever producer would have him. He recorded a follow-up song called "I'm Sorry" for Sir Cavaliers that was also unsuccessful commercially.

Cliff wanted to make another record, but after two misfires he didn't know who would take a chance on him. One night he was walking along a street when he passed a store that was closing up for the evening. It was Beverley's, an establishment that did triple duty as a restaurant, ice-cream parlor, and record shop. Cliff had an idea. Perhaps if he wrote a song about "Beverley's" he could convince the Chinese Jamaican owners—Leslie Kong and his two brothers—to record it. Cliff went home and wrote a song called "Dearest Beverley" and came back to the shop the next night. He asked, "Who's the boss?" and pushed his way in to see the owners. He told them he had a song for them and they told him that they only sold records, they didn't record them. Cliff sang his new song a cappella. Two of the brothers who ran the store started to laugh; Leslie Kong didn't laugh.

"I think I will go into this business," Kong said.

Cliff would say later: "And that was it, we went in together from there; he had the bread, I had the songs."

Cliff's first two songs for Count Boysie and Sir Cavaliers had been love songs. He decided he needed a new approach for his first recording for the newly established Beverley's Records. "I realized that wasn't where it was at if you wanted to sell records, you have to have something different, and my first real hit was called 'Hurricane Hattie,' which came from my third session," Cliff recalled. "There had been a hurricane in South America somewhere and I made a song about it, I was saying if you mess with me, I'll be like this hurricane. And that was a number one." Cliff also began to search out new talent for Kong. He was a star and a star maker, and he was only fourteen years old. About ten years later, in 1972, he would garner international acclaim as the lead in the film *The Harder They Come*.

As a talent scout for Leslie Kong, Cliff and Derrick Morgan, another scout for Kong, would hang out in a bar in West Kingston. They let the word spread: if singers wanted to try out for the Beverley's label, they knew where to find them. The singer would have to perform for Cliff on the spot, with no instruments or backup. That way Cliff could really tell if the person's voice was good and if the song was strong. And if he liked what he heard, he'd take the singer to see the boss—Leslie Kong.

Bob was still smarting from his first unexplained rejection from Leslie Kong. In the wake of Dekker's success, he wanted to try again. He sent a friend down to the bar where Cliff and Morgan were hanging out to tell the scouts about him. Cliff and Morgan sent the friend back and told him to tell Marley to come down himself. When Bob showed up, Morgan was gone. It was just Cliff—who was almost three years younger than Bob—sitting at the piano. He was working out a song.

"That sound good, y'know," said Bob.

It must have been a sight, and something to hear as well. Fourteen-year-old record executive Jimmy Cliff auditioning sixteen-year-old Bob Marley. Both were experienced well beyond their years. Cliff was struck by the fact that Bob didn't seem nervous at all. He quickly picked up on what Cliff was doing on the piano and how he was putting together verses and the chorus. Cliff recognized that Marley had instinctive musical talent, and had already had some training. It became clear that he hadn't come down in person before because he didn't want to be told no twice. Bob presented Cliff with five songs that he had written, and Cliff went through them and picked out the strongest three. A week or so later, Leslie Kong took Bob to Federal Studios to record his song.

"What if it a hit?" Bob asked Kong after the session was finished.

After Kong gave Bob a dismissive answer, Bob said he wanted out of the deal. A Kong strongman forced him to sign a release form, pushed Bob out of the studio, and he ran home—but not before he grabbed the acetates to his new recordings.

Cliff would say later that the trio of songs that Marley recorded for Kong in February 1962 represented his core identity as an artist. All three were ska songs, and all three were passionate and direct. "Judge Not" was a number about living life by one's own rules, and not passing judgment on the lives of others. It captured Bob's free spirit, and his eagerness to defy convention. Like much of Bob's work that was to follow, it was biblically inspired. Matthew, chapter 7, verse 1, reads: "Judge not, that ye not be judged"—the main theme of Marley's lyric. "One Cup of Coffee" was a love song, but it carried with it a hint of sadness. A pair of lovers has broken apart. Lawyers and payouts are involved. But at least on one side, love still remains. This song represented the romantic side of Bob. The last song that Bob recorded for that session was titled "Terror" and it reportedly dealt with rebellion. Bob would return to the themes he evoked at that recording session throughout his career.

All the songs, however, were commercial failures. "Judge Not" was released as Bob's first single under the name "Robert Marley." It was a flop. "One Cup of Coffee" was released next, under a name that was thought to be a little more commercial-sounding: "Bobby Martell." It received little airplay on the radio. "Terror" was apparently never pressed on record and no tapes of the song have surfaced since it was recorded.

It may have been best that "One Cup of Coffee" never became a hit, since Marley had copied virtually the entire song, without credit, from a 1961 hit by American singer/songwriter/guitarist Claude Gray. Country music has long had many fans in Jamaica. Patsy Cline songs were popular on Jamaican radio in the 1950s and 1960s, Johnny Cash built a home in Jamaica, and Willie Nelson recorded a reggae album late in his career. Gray, a six-foot five-inch country star nicknamed "the Tall Texan," scored his first Top Ten hit in 1960 with his song "The Family Bible." His next hit was "I'll Just Have a Cup of Coffee (Then I'll Go)," which was written by songwriter Bill Brock and entered the country Top Five in America. Gray was a deejay at a radio station in Meridian, Mississippi, in 1960 when he came across Brock's version of the song and decided to record it himself. "I'll Just Have a Cup of Coffee (Then I'll Go)" is about two lovers who are going their separate ways, and the lawyers and money that are complicating the breakup. The lyrics, with only a few word changes, are virtually the same as in Marley's version. There's a line in each song about bringing money to a lawyer, a passage about kissing sleeping kids, and a section comparing the warmth and sweetness of coffee to an ex-lover's arms. Gray contests: "It's the same song." On the original Beverley's Records 45, the only songwriter credited is "R. Marley." A re-release of the track on the Bob Marley *Songs of Freedom* boxed set in 1992 also credits the song to "Robert Marley." Plagiarism aside, it's a sign of his willingness to cross cultural boundaries that one of his very first musical recordings in Jamaica was based on a country song from America.

It may be that the failure to credit the real songwriter behind "One Cup of Coffee" wasn't Bob's fault at all. Jamaican singers regularly covered American hit songs without the original sources being credited. Jamaican record companies were tightfisted enough about giving the proper credit and payments to Jamaican musicians, much less foreigners, who were, in all likelihood, not even aware that they were being cheated out of a check. It is a tribute to Bob that as his career developed he moved away from copying the songs of others and began focusing on material that he had composed. After 1972, he almost never recorded other people's compositions.

There are different reports on how much Bob got paid for his first session with Kong. All the accounts agree that it wasn't very much. Bob would later say that he got paid two ten-pound notes. His mother remembers it as five pounds, out of which he gave her two. Bob wasn't happy with Kong and the way he handled the session and the release of his first singles. He also didn't think much of Kong as a producer. Said Bob: "Well, I don't know what to say about Leslie Kong because he didn't really know anything about music. He used to jus' sit down and listen and if the music was good he would say yes it's nice; if not, he'd make you play it over again. He was just a lucky guy because he had the money. He got some big hits as soon as he started from Jimmy [Cliff], Monty Morris, and Derrick Morgan and he made all the money."

Years later, after Bob became a star, Kong decided to revisit his recordings with Marley. He announced that he would release a new album, based on that material, titled *The Best of the Wailers*. Bunny Wailer, hearing of the plan, is said to have confronted Kong at Beverley's.

"Don' do it, mon," he said to Kong. "It cannot be de best of de Wailers, 'cause our best is yet ta come. When yuh seh dat de best of someone has done, den dat person is already dead or soon dyin', so we don' wan' dat."

Kong started to answer, but Bunny would have none of it.

Said Bunny: "If yuh do dis t'ing I prophesize dat it is yuh who will die."

Kong had the album printed up anyway and it was a runaway hit in Jamaica. Several weeks later, Kong's accountant came by his office to tell him he was officially a millionaire. Kong went home early, complaining that he felt ill. Hours later, he died of a heart attack. Kong had had no previous history of heart problems.

Marley decided it was time to form a group. As a solo singer, he was out fighting for his work alone. He was at the mercy of producers who were determined to squeeze performers dry and pay them as little as possible. If Bob had a group, he would have support. Said Bob: "Well, you're always growing. In Jamaica there is plenty friends you know. So I don't feel like going down the street and singing alone. So me and my friend go down the street and he sing on top. When we sing we're not individualists. We like whoever's around to do it with us. You know what I mean? They were just me friends."

Bunny was the first person he approached about starting a group. Said Bob: "My greatest influence at the time was the Drifters—'Magic Moment,' 'Please Stay,' those things. So I figured I should get a group together." Bunny was hesitant. He had composed a song called "Pass It On"—which would later go on to become a reggae classic—and was going to record it at the same

Beverley's session that Bob had gone to and recorded "Judge Not." But because Bunny could not get out of school that day, Kong had canceled his session. Bunny didn't like the way the record producers treated artists. He wasn't certain that he wanted to get pulled into that world. His family already had a future mapped out for him, and had sacrificed much to give him a chance to get an education in America. Bob's idea sounded too risky. Bunny was doing well in his classes. He had won a scholarship to attend Camperdown High School. He didn't want to walk away from his educational accomplishments. Says Bunny: "I was still attending school, I was getting ready to go to college, I was getting ready to go to Howard University [a historically black university in Washington, D.C.] when Bob urged me to start dealing with singing. I had a brother attending [Howard] at the time. He graduated with a bachelor of arts. He was there paving the way for me to take over after he left when Bob came by with this music thing, which was something I really loved to do. But my parents were not enthused on that. They wanted me to be a doctor or a lawyer or something. My intentions were to go to university until Bob kept telling me I was the one who got him involved. He just kept on keeping on like that until I decided, okay, what else am I gonna do?"

Bob's passion and hounding won Bunny over. Both Bunny and Bob agreed that if they were going to pursue a career in music, the venture couldn't be a lark. They were both giving up too much not to treat their new profession seriously. They would have to plan. This was to be a well-run moneymaking operation. They would have to select the other members of the group carefully. The radio provided them with inspiration for the sort of band they wanted to put together. Bob wanted them to be a vocal group. He wanted to follow in the footsteps of the Platters, Little Anthony and the Imperials, the Drifters, and Frankie Lymon and the Teenagers. They considered several names for the group before settling on the Teenagers. They were all teenagers and they admired Frankie Lymon, so it made sense. Soon the name was changed to something less derivative: the Wailing Rudeboys, the Wailing Wailers, and then simply the Wailers. Over the years the group members gave many and varying explanations for the group's final name. It was Trench Town itself that really named the Wailers. The group's members heard wailing all around them—from the old, from the sick, from babies, from sufferers. The group was wailing because they were being cheated—by record companies, by society, by the government. Plus Bunny thought the word evoked something religious—the Wailing Wall of Jerusalem. The name signaled that this was a group with serious intentions. They weren't just entertaining, they weren't just singing—they were wailing. A serious group needed serious singers. "We recruited members who we thought could have been capable, but after testing them and going through certain processing they weren't capable of taking the journey," Bunny remembers. "We were serious about doing this because we were abandoning stuff that our parents had provided for us to be something that they didn't plan for and we didn't plan for either. We had to [recruit] the right members to make it the kind of group that could be professional."

Winston Hubert McIntosh was the only son of Alvera Coke. He was one of many children born to his father, James McIntosh, who may have had more than a dozen babies by various women. Tosh was born in the Grange Hill district in the parish of Hanover on October 19, 1944. He was left by his parents with an aunt at the age of three. Said Tosh: "I didn't live with my mother, but I am my mother's only child, and I didn't grow with her, I was grown with my aunt, my mother's aunt, my grand-aunt, when I was three years old until I was fifteen."

Tosh claimed that neither his parents, nor his aunt, had much influence on his life. "See, I was three years in size, but fifty years old in the mind, see?" said Tosh. "I was born, raised in righteousness, not to say that my parents were righteous, because they did not know what was righteousness. They were being led away to a sh–tstem, or being deceived by deceivers, you see, because they wanted to know what was righteousness." His relatives were extremely religious Christians and would take him to church once every day, twice on Sunday. He attended Savanna La Mar Comprehensive School in Westmoreland. He later migrated to Denham Town in Kingston with his aunt to start an apprenticeship as a welder. When his aunt died, he went to live with an uncle in Trench Town. He was a tall young man, over six feet five inches. He loved carving, fishing, diving, martial arts, and music. He was blunt spoken and didn't turn away from confrontation or run from fights. He saw himself as a man of the people, but he reveled in standing out from the crowd. Many Jamaicans rode bicycles around Kingston. Tosh would regularly use a unicycle. Said Tosh: "I was born like many others, in the country, and came into the shitty. Live in Trench Town. Met Bob and Bunny and some others yout's and we sing together. In the same ghetto, in the same life, being oppressed in the same way."

Peter was the kind of person who was not so much unafraid to speak his mind as he was unable not to do so. He renamed the world around him, turning "oppressors" into "downpressors," "the system" in "the sh–tstem," and "Kingston" in "Killsome." He had a rage boiling up in him—heated by his difficult upbringing, the poverty he saw around him, and his frustration with religious institutions—that he could not contain. He tried, at various times, to cool the rage—by presenting it in soothing song, or in the context of humor. On occasion, he let his boiling ire simmer down into a bitter humor. More often than not, he just didn't care.

Heated words would pour out of him like hot water from a kettle tipped to one side. He didn't care if the boiling rage went in the cup or splashed and scalded someone at the table. On the "Red X" tapes, he describes "killsome" as "the pit of hell."

Peter lived on West Road and Bob and Bunny lived nearby on Second Street. One day in 1962, Bunny approached him about Bob's idea.

"Bwoy, I want form a group," Bunny said.

"How you mean, me ready, man," replied Tosh.

Tosh had a reputation around Trench Town as an instrumentalist. "He could sing and play the guitar," said Bunny. "I knew he would be a very effective member of the group, being able to play the guitar as well as sing. That's what Trench Town was—there were a lot of kids and a lot of talent and you could always pick from these multitalented kids whenever you wanted to, whether it was football, cricket, sports, or entertainment."

Tosh had been interested in music since childhood. His mother sang in church and he would join her. He would remember this as his first exposure to music. He was only two years old. True to his character, he viewed his early musical experience through the prism of politics. "Well, I was born into a world of white supremacy," said Tosh. "I went to church to learn to sing 'Lord wash me and I shall be whiter than snow.' Those were the kind of things that created inferiority complex." A few years later, he began to focus on the songs he heard on the radio. Said Tosh: "Well, when I was five years old there was plenty country-and-western music on the air and Elvis Presley and all those kind of music. All ancient white pop or rock artists we used to hear. I used to hear them plenty on the radio. But I was not influenced by that music." Instead his musical influences were primarily American soul stars—Curtis Mayfield, Otis Redding, Al Green, and James Brown. Despite his tough exterior, he had a soft side. Tosh would later list his favorite composer as Thom Bell ("Betchy By Golly Wow"), his favorite album as the Stylistics' *Round Two*, and his favorite song as Roberta Flack's "Killing Me Softly."

When Tosh was five years old, he made his first guitar. He built it out of a piece of board, fishing line, and a sardine tin. Said Tosh: "And I even tuned it myself without even asking somebody to tune it, and I played it. People used to throw pennies, because it sounded good. It was a concept of creativity that was in me for some time." Soon after that, his mother sent him for music lessons. Said Tosh: "I was born a musician, see. And after I learned to play guitar, my mother send me to piano lessons and I did that for about eight months. And when I did it for about six months the woman say she never seen anyone—she teaches many people to play the piano—she never seen anyone who learn the music so quick, see." Tosh soon turned away from the piano and back to the guitar. "I was so overwhelmed and enthusiastic over how the guitar sound. And I just put piano back behind and start to get into the rhythm guitar because I thought there was something very effective in the rhythm with guitar. And I loved it from that. It was like it was part piano."

When Tosh was twelve, a local man gave him some instruction in guitar. "How I learned my guitar is I was at the house, at my mother's house [in Westmoreland], and there was an old man who used to live up the road who could play some nice country-western style and some church music. And when he came to my gate one day he was picking his guitar and I just liked the way he was picking his guitar, and I just came near . . . And it was the first time I got hold of a professional guitar."

Three other members were recruited for the group. One was Franklin Delano Alexander Braithwaite (known as Junior) who lived on Third Street when Bob lived on Second Street: "As children, we had something in common because we loved singing."

Another was a female singer, Beverly Kelso: "I was about sixteen at the time and performin' in what we used to call 'fun clubs.' This one club was a place on Wellington Road that teenage people could go to in the early evenin' to dance and show their talent. It was about three P.M. and I was singin' down the aisle of the club when Bob walked in and saw me. After my song he came right over and asked if I wanted to sing with his group. I started laughin' and he said, 'Nuh, I'm serious!' So I told him, 'Anytime you're ready.'" Another singer, Cherry Green, was recruited to fill out the band. Cherry's real name was Ermine Bramwell, but her reddish skin gained her the nickname Cherry. Her father died when she was young, so she went by the last name of her brother, which was Green. She was older than the other Wailers—a relatively ancient nineteen, and thus almost out of her teenage years. She had a young child and a job sewing at a local bra factory. She was singing an American song outside her house in Trench Town on Second Street when a neighbor, Joe Higgs, passed by.

"Cherry, tat you?" Higgs asked, pleased and intrigued by the sweet mystery voice.

"Yes!" she replied.

Higgs went to tell Bob about what he had heard, and Cherry became a Wailer. She would never have predicted that she would be in a band with someone like Bob. Said Cherry: "We used to call him little white boy because he had curly hair, y'know? Soft curly hair." The original Wailers were now complete.

The fledgling group wanted to record immediately. The top producer at the time was Clement "Coxson" Dodd, the founder of Studio One. The Wailers wanted to get an audience with Coxson. They wanted to record at Studio One, but they needed guidance. They found a mentor in Joe Higgs. "My greatest influence is a Rasta guy called Joe Higgs," Bob would say later. Bunny echoed:

"Joe Higgs himself had his own duo group—Higgs & Wilson, that what he was singing as when we knew him. We knew him as a star, not as a tutor. But he took time out to train the Wailers because he saw where there was some talent inside of the Wailers and his contribution could make it better." Higgs had been taking note of Bob and Bunny and offering his counsel even before the two launched their group. "Bob Marley was on Second Street and I was on Third Street," Higgs recalled. "Bob and Bunny Livingston were living in Bunny's father Toddy's house with Cedella, Bob's mother. A guy by the name of Errol, whose father was a man who had a scrap-iron yard on Spanishtown Road and Bread Lane near Back o' Wall, used to tell me he'd like me to teach Bob Marley to sing and play music. So Bob and I started to hang out before the Wailers were even conceived."

Higgs was born June 3, 1940, in Jamaica. His mother's family hailed from Maroon Town in St. Thomas. As a teen, he listened to Louis Jordan, Louis Armstrong, Billy Eckstine, Matt Munro, Mario Lanza, and Cuban mambo and ballads. His mother taught him to sing. He would follow her to church meetings. He was fascinated by the way she would sing a song and find fresh harmonies. He couldn't believe that his mother could sound like Mahalia Jackson. In her voice, he found his own. He performed in amateur talent shows around Kingston in the 1950s with limited success until he met up with Roy Wilson. They became partners. They came in second during their initial performance together, but then ran off with so many first-place titles in a row they were barred from amateur competitions because they were considered professionals. After one show at the Ward Theatre in Kingston, Higgs found a man waiting for him outside.

"Were you the guy who was singing onstage?" said the man.

"Yes," Higgs said.

"The crowd loved that song. I want to record that song."

The man was Edward Seaga, a Jamaican music producer. He recorded Higgs & Wilson's song "Manny-O" in 1959 and it became an islandwide hit. Seaga later went into politics and became prime minister of Jamaica.

Higgs was well aware that the music industry was a rat race. He tried to do all he could to help younger singers along. His yard in Trench Town was an open-air university of sound, and young vocalists were welcome to stop by and learn from the master. Higgs said he taught "harmony, structuring sound, and the consciousness of sound . . . What I was doing was sharing, giving freely of what I knew."

He saw talent in the Wailers, but he also thought they needed work. He was searching for harmony. Just as his mother had found fresh harmonies in church, he wanted to find them in the Wailers' music. He wanted precision. He demanded hard work. It was only through effort that the performance would seem effortless. Each Wailer had to be a leader. Each had to be able to wail and to stand out in a crowd. So Higgs would bring the Wailers to his yard night after night. Sometimes it was just the Wailers. Other times singers from around Trench Town would join in, some professional and some not. Every night was a new challenge, a new sound, and a new search for harmony and precision.

Bob learned how to let his vocals express emotion naturally, without forcing sentiment into a song. "Me like meself better when I just sing," said Bob, "more than trying to sing. Because you're singing something fast, then you have to depend on your voice to sing it. If you sing something real, then you sing it on your own. If I just sing a love song now, I depend upon a sweet voice to sing it. Singing something real, you don't sing it because you really see it and you mean it, so you don't have no sweet way to sing it. You could almost talk it."

Higgs also taught Bob to appreciate different forms of music.

"Den I go down into Trench Town and start listening to jazz, 'cept me couldn't understand it," Bob said. "Afta while I smoke some ganja, some herb, and get to understand it. Me try to get into de mood where de moon is blue and see de feelin' expressed. Joe Higgs 'elped me understand that music. 'E taugh me many t'ings."

The group began to show improvement on lead vocals and harmonies. Friends and well-wishers who had stopped by the Wailers' practice sessions thought they were ready to record and that it was time to bring them to Studio One. Higgs didn't think the Wailers were ready. He had another approach in mind. His strategy was for the group to tour areas outside of Trench Town. He wanted to introduce them to the public and strengthen the group's confidence. He also wanted to study the response of the crowd and see what other things needed to be worked on.

After the live performances, Higgs pronounced the group ready. It was time to meet Sir Coxson at Studio One.

SLAVE DRIVER

I magine you are there, on midnight on Sunday, August 5, 1962, as Jamaica celebrates its first Independence Day. You see citizens of the new nation marking the occasion by lowering the red, white, and blue Union Jack in parishes around the island. Then you see them raise the black, gold, and green Jamaican flag. Church bells are tolled in Port Antonio and elsewhere. There is singing and shouts of joy in the streets of every city and town. Roadside vendors hawk treats like plantain tarts, banana loaf, and coconut drops. There are speeches and parades around the island. In the roadways of Ocho Rios, children and adults perform Jonkanoo dances (a colorful and energetic form of revelry with roots that reach back to Africa). In Bob Marley's home parish of St. Ann, bonfires can be seen burning on the peaks of the Blue Mountains and fireworks are set off over cricket grounds. Three hundred years of British rule have ended. Everyone is overjoyed. Nobody knows what will happen next.

On the streets of Jamaica's capital, Bob Marley was witnessing the start of a new revolution. This was a cultural civil war, pitting the past against the future, the old against the young, and a fresh form of musical expression against everything that had gone before. Bob would become the insurrection's guiding spirit. In June of 1950, Jamaica launched its own Kingston-based commercial broadcasting entity: Radio Jamaica Rediffusion Ltd., a.k.a. RJR. In 1959, it was joined by another station, the Jamaica Broadcasting Corporation, a.k.a. JBC. Both radio broadcasters were government owned and operated. The music they played tended to be jazz, classical, and gospel—a step or two behind what younger Jamaicans wanted to hear. And, in any case, many Jamaicans couldn't afford radios. For them, RJR and JBC were invisible, inaudible, and irrelevant.

The sound of the island was changing. The slave era had seen the spread of Jonkanoo, with its rattles, drumming, conch-shell blowing, and bands of masqueraders dressed as animals or devils. In the early twentieth century, Jamaican workers returning home from work on the Panama Canal and elsewhere brought to the island the sound of calypso, samba, and tango and helped to create mento, a rural dance music with sexy and playful lyrics. In the 1940s, Jamaicans visiting America came back with "race records," and public appetite for rhythm and blues began to increase. But with radios, records, and record players priced too high for the average Jamaican to buy, another way was needed to get the music to the people. The sound-system wars had begun.

The first sound systems emerged in Jamaica in the 1950s. They were crude, rickety contraptions, usually made up of belt-driven turntables perched on homemade amplifiers, with a transistor radio wired in to carry the midrange and the treble. Soon the sound systems became more sophisticated and powerful. They could be heard rumbling out their tunes several streets away. Music lovers picked their favorite system operators, jilted them, and were wooed back. Sound-system dances attracted more than six hundred people at a time, with hundreds more clamoring outside. They were held at places like Forrester's Hall at 21 North Street in Kingston. Revelers would sway to the music on the dance floor, or drink rum at the bar and eat curried goat. The lower reaches of Kingston's Orange Street were renamed Beat Street and the boom of the new kings of music echoed around the city. Huge outdoor parties would be held at various "lawns"—King's Lawn on North Street, Chocomo Lawn on Wellington Street, Bull Head Lawn on Central Road in Trench Town. Sound-system operators became superstars, and bestowed on themselves stage names with lofty royal titles—King Edwards, Prince Buster, Duke Vin. (They were following in the footsteps of calypso singers, who often dubbed themselves dukes or counts.) The handpicked "selectors"—the deejays charged with spinning the records at the dances—honed their showmanship skills, arriving at dances in black leather Dracula capes, white Lone Ranger masks, and cardboard crowns.

Of all the players to emerge from the sound-system wars of the late 1950s and 1960s, two stood above the rest: Arthur Reid, a.k.a. Duke Reid, and Clement Dodd, a.k.a. Sir Coxson Downbeat.

Reid was the older man, and had entered the music business first. He was born in 1915 in Jamaica and worked as a policeman in Kingston for a decade. In the 1950s, he and his wife, Lucille, bought the Treasure Island liquor store. To attract customers, Reid began hosting a radio program called *Treasure Island Time* and playing American R&B records. Sound systems were just then growing in popularity, so Reid started his own, which he called the Trojan. As an ex-policeman, he had a reputation for toughness and he reveled in it. He became known for carrying a pair of revolvers on his waist and wearing an ermine cape and a gold crown. He would appear at a sound-system dance sitting on a throne carried in by four sturdy cronies. He was said to have once studied obeah, which he would purportedly employ to take out his enemies. Starting a rumor that you have studied dark magic is almost as good as actually knowing some.

Coxson, born in 1932 in Kingston, got his moniker for his all-around skills at cricket as a youth. (Alec Coxson was the name of a popular Yorkshire cricketer in the 1940s.) In the wake of a great hurricane that hit Jamaica in 1951, Coxson traveled to Florida to work on the farms. Once there, he fell in love with American rhythm and blues. He traveled America in search of work and music. "At that time, we were in search of boogie-woogie, good jazz, merengue, stuff like that," Coxson once recalled. "I was lucky enough to find a lot of music in Brooklyn, and from there on, I made regular visits to New York and Chicago." His mother ran a grocery store back home, so he began sending her back records. She would play them to attract customers to the shop. When Coxson returned to the island, he brought with him stacks of American releases from the likes of Billy Eckstine, Sarah Vaughan, T-Bone Walker, Lionel Hampton, B.B. King, and Louis Jordan. People began to come from all around Kingston to sit outside the shop and listen to the music, and soon Coxson launched his own sound system.

One of Coxson's innovations was to encourage the use of "toasting," witty patter that deejays or "selectors" would employ between songs and even over songs to energize crowds. Coxson had a peculiar sense of humor. He was given to making the kinds of jokes that didn't make people laugh or smile—his brand of humor raised eyebrows. He was a quiet man, even courtly, but had a famously strange habit of calling everyone he met "Jackson." He liked to call himself "Scorcher" and adopted it as his songwriting pseudonym. He was also savagely competitive, loving to win as much as he liked making the other guy lose. Duke Reid's family and Coxson's family were on friendly terms. When Coxson saw Reid in the street, he would give him a friendly "Hello, Mr. Reid." On one occasion, after he had passed Reid on the street and exchanged pleasantries, Coxson turned to an associate and confided: "I'm going to damage him musically."

Coxson's mean streak found expression in toasting. Sometimes toasters would boast about their abilities. Other times they would savage the competition. Nobody was safe from the barbs—people in the audience, workers behind the bar, even the artists on the records on the turntables. Anyone could spin a record, if you had the money to buy a turntable and a 45. Toasting made each spin of a record unique; it turned a dance party into a performance; it made deejays verbal gladiators and transformed music into a blood sport. Toasting allowed Coxson to employ his eccentric wit and to indulge his lust for competition. Count Machuki, Dodd's first deejay, lays claim to inventing the form in the 1950s. He was deejaying in front of a crowd that needed a boost. The way Machuki remembers it, he told Coxson to "give me the microphone." Then Machuki went to work, making wisecracks, with Coxson urging him on, and even supplying him with a few lines.

Coxson and Machuki realized they were onto something. Others would follow. King Stitt, another Coxson selector, points out that "Coxson wasn't the first sound system. But Coxson's sound system was the first sound system to create disc jockeys that would use the microphone in between records. All the other deejays before our time would just put on a record and either dance with a girl, or drink a beer, but it wasn't anything exciting." Coxson once boasted: "I was the first rapper."

The young Wailers—Bob, Peter, Bunny, Junior, Beverly, and Cherry—couldn't help but hear the echo of the sound systems. Beverly was a teenager living on Fifth Street and Central Road in

Trench Town in the 1960s. The area was poor, but it was not the gangland it would become a decade later. Her family would sleep with the apartment door open, to let the breeze blow in and to better hear the music on the street. On Friday and Saturday nights she would go to dance halls and hear selectors like King Stitt. She could feel the thump of the music, see glimpses of the swirling dancers, even smell the mix of sweat and curry and alcohol coming from inside the dance hall—but she was only a kid then, so they wouldn't let her in. So she would stay outside with the other youngsters. Sometimes they stayed outside all night. But they never got tired. The music kept their feet and their eyelids light.

Throughout the 1950s and 1960s, Duke Reid and Sir Coxson clashed repeatedly in battles that were part of an epic musical war. They would set up camp on the opposite sides of a lawn, each trying to lure the crowd away from the other. They would greedily hunt down the latest records from America and scratch the names off of the labels so their rivals couldn't track down the same hits. Coxson renamed Willis Jackson's "Later for Gator" as "Coxson's Hop." He made it his theme song and kept its true name concealed for years. Both sound-system operators traveled with enforcers. Cecil Campbell, a.k.a. Prince Buster, was a former amateur boxer who was first hired by the Coxson camp after deejay Count Machuki saw him with a knife in his hand chasing down one of Duke Reid's henchmen. Prince Buster would go on to launch his own sound system, "Voice of the People," and become a recording star. He made an impression on Bob, who considered him one of his favorite performers.

In 1959, after years of warfare, Coxson hatched a new strategy. He wanted to stop imitating the sounds of America. He wanted to launch a truly Jamaican sound. So he held a meeting to discuss it. It was akin to Berry Gordy calling a meeting to decide what would succeed the Motown sound, or Sam Phillips sitting down with associates at Sun Records to plan the next step after rock and roll. Gordy and Phillips never held such meetings—deep cultural shifts are rarely dictated from conference rooms. They usually involve taking advantage, impromptu, of changing popular tastes. Sparking a fad is one thing, engineering a cultural movement is another.

Coxson, however, had a different approach. He couldn't wait around for the public to decide what it wanted. He was a businessman and he wanted to make money immediately. He met with Ernest Ranglin and bass player Cluett "Clue-J" Johnson at a liquor store on Love Lane. They came up with a sound that would reach beyond the shuffle boogie rhythms popularized by American acts like Louis Jordan and Erskine Hawkins. The new music would be called ska (the name was an onomatopoetic choice). The next morning, Coxson went down to JBC Radio's studios and recorded "Easy Snappin'." The record featured Theophilus Beckford as lead vocalist, Clue-J on bass, Roland Alphonso on tenor sax, and was arranged by Ranglin. "Playing the shuffle beat, it was always on the downbeat, so we were trying to see if we could find something different, like an identity for ourselves," explains Ranglin. "So we figured we would try the downbeat on the second beat. If you notice, all the emphasis is always on the second beat of the music. So at first it may feel a little awkward, but eventually you'll find you'll get used to it."

People got used to it fast. "Easy Snappin'" was a smash and is regarded by many as the first ska record. The new music was fast, pointed, and carefree. It caused feet to move and heart rates to race. It was a hormonal sound, evoking pelvic thrusts and pumping fists. It was youthful impatience set to a beat. Ranglin would later arrange and perform on the first worldwide ska hit, "My Boy Lollipop" by Millie Small, which hit number two on the British charts in 1964, and was Top Five in the United States. Coxson saw there was a future in recording local artists. A nightclub named The End in Kingston was closing down. "When they folded, we said, 'we're gonna make it the beginning instead of the end,'" Coxson joked. In 1962, he opened up his own recording studio at the site and dubbed it the Jamaica Recording and Publishing Studio. He handpicked the best musicians from the local orchestras to come record at his new site. Coxson's recording venture was a huge success. He helped launch the careers of Ranglin, trombonist Don Drummond, Toots and the Maytals, and many others, including the Skatalites, who functioned as a house band. Soon his venture became known by a new name: Studio One. Coxson was no longer simply spinning records, he was making them. The sound-system wars had entered a new era.

You may think that rap and reggae come from different worlds. You may think that they speak in different voices, and move to different beats. While Bob sang of "One Love," rappers like Snoop Dogg call for "187 on an undercover cop." While Bob crooned to "Turn Your Lights Down Low," rappers like Kanye West accuse women of being "Gold Diggers." But the same forces that helped create reggae also created rap. Bob was singing about the "Concrete Jungle" long before American rappers had bought their first turntables. And many rap pioneers heard the records of the Jamaican sound-system warriors before they went on to make their own recordings. Hip-hop may have been born in the Bronx, but it was conceived in Kingston.

DJ Kool Herc, a.k.a. Clive Campbell—considered the godfather of rap—was born in Jamaica's capital city. He grew up in Trench Town and used to haunt the same yards where the Wailers practiced their music. He would linger outside of sound-system dances in the early 1960s, hungry to get in, but too young to gain entrance. You suspect he would have had to cross paths with the Wailers at some point. He says he used to walk some of the same streets—First Street and Second Street. He probably knew some of the same people. He no doubt heard some of the same music, booming out of storefronts and churches. When Herc moved to the United States in the late 1960s at the age of twelve, he would take what he saw and heard on the island of Jamaica and bring it to the island of Manhattan. Herc is credited with pioneering the practice of rapping over instrumental breaks at Bronx parties in the 1970s.

Many of rap's founding figures have Caribbean roots. Afrika Bambaataa, who introduced drum machines and synthesizers to rap, was born to parents of Jamaican and Barbadian descent. Grandmaster Flash—who recorded the classic song "The Message" with his group the Furious Five—was born in Barbados. Voletta Wallace, the mother of Christopher Wallace, a.k.a. the Notorious B.I.G., the greatest of all the gangsta rap MCs, was born in the parish of Trelawny on Jamaica's North Coast. Wallace later moved to Kingston and lived there during the same period in the 1960s when the Wailers were forging their sound.

It is no coincidence that the founding figures of rap and the King of Reggae shared the same Caribbean incubator. Many residents of the Bronx originally came from the West Indies. The deejay culture that inspired Marley also inspired the leading purveyors of hip-hop. (One of RUN-D.M.C.'s early songs, "Roots, Rap, Reggae," celebrates the shared history of the genres and borrowed its title from a Marley number, "Roots, Rock, Reggae.") The passion and innovation that went into creating rap is inseparable from the elements that went into launching the Wailers. Rap and reggae were separated by the Caribbean Sea but by little else. It's not that long a journey from Nine Miles to Eminem's Eight Mile. Some of the artists who recorded at Studio One would have been right at home on Death Row. The mix of guns and ganja, turntables and rebellion, that formed the core of Bob's story served as the blueprint for the hip-hoppers that followed him. Jamaican toasting and American rapping are different names for the same form of expression. Only Bob's accent was different. Not his Jamaican accent. His accent on life.

Studio One was located at 13 Brentford Road in Kingston. Bob, Bunny, Peter, Beverly, Cherry, and Junior were anxious and excited as they showed up for their first audition as a band. Bob gave this take on Coxson: "Him have the best studio during that time . . . Not the best equipment, but the best vibe." Higgs and Alvin "Seeco" Patterson, a friend of the band, also accompanied the youngsters for support. Bunny recalls that it was a Sunday night in December 1963. Regular studio hours during the weekdays were 10 A.M. to 4 P.M. On Saturdays and Sundays performers would often stop by to lay down vocals and the sessions could go late into the evenings. The grounds outside Studio One were typically packed with musicians, singers, and would-be entertainers. There were also residents from the area peeking around, just hoping to hear some good music or to meet up with one of their favorite performers. Many performers had day jobs. They would come down to the studio for a recording session, then head back to their workplaces. Behind the studio there were fruit trees bearing ackee, breadfruit, limes, and oranges. Artists who were not actively involved in a session were drafted to "run the boat" or do some cooking for the others. The air outside was laced with the smell of roasting breadfruit and the aroma of ganja. The employees at Studio One sometimes felt as if they were running a kind of triage unit separating out the talented from the untalented, just as doctors divide the sick and the healthy. After an act's audition for Coxson, he would sometimes cry out: "Next patient!"

Bob and his companions walked through Studio One, aware of all the talent around them. There were a lot of great vocalists—the Wailers could hear them warming up their voices. Some of them would have cut their eyes at the Wailers. Who did these youngsters think they were? What made them think they had the talent to record for Studio One? Everyone was waiting for an audience with Coxson. Everyone was waiting for that big break. Most people would go home with nothing—no record, no deal, and no dreams. Bob, with his old, ill-fitting clothes, big nose, and skinny body, didn't look like a pop idol. With his high, sharp voice and country-bwoy accent, he didn't sound like a hit maker. What was he doing here at Studio One, where stars were launched?

The Wailers went into the audition room. It turned out to be the studio itself. On a tall bench at the north end of the studio was Coxson. He looked down on the newcomers like a pharaoh on a throne, dressed simply in slacks and a jacket. He was also wearing a questioning frown. It was not an inviting gaze. He seemed to want to intimidate the people who came before him. The recording business was not for the faint of heart. This was a trial by fire and he was the chief judge and flamethrower. If the Wailers couldn't take the heat, it was time for them to get out of Studio One.

The Wailers started their set. Peter played an acoustic guitar while the others sang. Together, they performed four songs: "Straight and Narrow Way," "I'm Going Home," "Do You Remember?," and "I Don't Need Your Love." The last song was Bob's newest composition. It was the one that he thought would win over the master of Studio One. Coxson seemed to enjoy what he heard. But he didn't seem blown away. The group needed to do more if they were going to make the audition a success.

"Bob, mek we do 'Simmer Down'?" Peter asked.

It was a song that Bob had written two years before. The group used it as a warm-up number, and Bob still didn't consider it a completed work. In fact, he was tired of it. Still, Seeco had heard the song before and liked it. Maybe it was worth playing it and taking a chance. Peter started playing the chords and the group went into the song.

"Simmer Down" was a generational anthem. It captured the spirit of freedom of postcolonial Jamaica and it distilled the sense of rebelliousness that had been brewing among the new nation's youth. And yet the song made no overt claims to weightiness. Its lyrics were deceptively simple. They spoke of nanny goats, hawks, and merry chickens. Bunny said the song was nothing more than a nursery rhyme, a pop trifle that drew on chants the band had heard in school yards. But its modest surface was part of its power. "Songs evolve," Bob once theorized. "There are songs I don't really understand until I see the reactions they lead to in the streets. Someone else finds out their meaning, and I understand it in turn." "Simmer Down" combined gentle country proverbs with a driving urban beat. The lyrics were sung in the local language—not the Queen's English—and that separated the song from American and British pop. It was something uniquely Jamaican—a musical declaration of independence. The song employed a local beat—ska—and that stamped it as something thrillingly indigenous. The number's call to "simmer down" and to "control your temper" could be interpreted as talking directly to the nation's youth, many of whom, at the time, were involved in escalating confrontations with police. For Jamaicans, "Simmer Down" carried with it the same cultural thrill that the Beatles' "I Want to Hold Your Hand" and Bob Dylan's "Like a Rolling Stone" had for Americans. The music was the epicenter of a youthquake.

Coxson had heard enough.

"Stop, all right," said Coxson. "No more."

He had halted the group after two verses of "Simmer Down." Was something wrong? Had the group, after all their hard work, blown the audition?

Coxson winked at Seeco, the man who had brought the band to his attention. Everything was all right. Coxson thought "Simmer Down" was a hit. It had the passion of youth, but it was also intelligent. The song could help Coxson win his next sound-system clash. He wanted the group to come back to record the tune, as well as the other songs they had sung for him that day. Coxson signed the Wailers to an exclusive contract. They would be paid a salary of three pounds a week. There was no talk of royalties.

The recording session was to take place the next day, Monday morning. Dawn couldn't come quick enough for the Wailers. Said Bunny: "I tossed, turned, and waited in my bed watching the clock and anticipating." The group met up on Monday for their usual rehearsal. They typically met in one of the yards in Trench Town. There was a feeling among all of them that something had changed. "We all had the feeling of being transferred to another grade to experience new pupils, teachers, and subjects," Bunny remembers.

It was time to head back to Studio One to make their first record as a group. Cherry would miss the event because of work. Things were happening fast. Beverly described the scene: "When I got there we had ten minutes' rehearsal, and Bob just had me doin' this chorus of 'simmer down, simmer down,' over and over behind him." They were soon summoned to the recording area. There, they found the members of the Skatalites waiting for them. The stellar guitarist Ernest Ranglin also joined the Wailers for those first sessions. The Wailers were overjoyed. The Skatalites were known as some of the best musicians on the island and Ernest Ranglin was the best guitarist in the Jamaican music business. The group had backed up many of the top musicians of the ska era, including the Maytals, Jackie Opel, and Delroy Wilson. They were regular headliners in local clubs and hotels. Inspired by the space race, drummer Lloyd Knibb had suggested a name for the group: "Satellites."

Saxophonist Tommy McCook replied: "No, we play ska—the Skatalites."

Having the Skatalites play backup on the Wailers record was an honor and an opportunity. It was also the usual way that Studio One did business, matching younger artists with veteran entertainers. Explains Dodd: "Most of the artists who came to me were fresh and young, they loved singing, but they had no musical background or experience, so the older, established artists had to help them." Working with musicians of such high caliber made the members of the Wailers feel like they were true professionals, not just teens on a lark. Their labor had paid off. They were working with the best and they could become the best themselves. When Bunny met the Skatalites that day, the word that came to his mind was *legendary*.

Ranglin was used to working with neophytes. Born in Manchester, Jamaica, he had moved to Kingston as a young man. He had helped invent ska, but he was rooted in jazz. His musical heroes were Charlie Christian, Django Reinhardt, Joe Pass, Red Norvo, and local musicians Don Hitchman, Cecil Houdini, and Collash. Ranglin had been working with Coxson for years, even before he opened Studio One. He worked as the house guitarist, as an arranger, composer, scout, and as a solo recording artist. He had auditioned so many acts, he couldn't remember all their names, even the ones that had gone on to successful music careers. Ranglin described a typical session this way: "I would check the artists and see what they have, and if [Coxson] wasn't going to be around, he would tell me check this guy because he seemed to have good potential or whatever it may be. So we used to check them out, like rehearse them but without any instruments or anything, so they would just sing and we could figure out from what we heard what we could do with them. Well, you know, whatever we always do, we hope—it's not like we think this is just another tune. In those days, records had an A side and a B side. We treat every song like an A side."

Coxson had started Studio One as a one-track studio with an Ampex 350. He tended to use a lot of microphones and often had wires and cords dangling from his hands. Recording sessions were mixed into mono recordings through Coxson's two six-channel Lang boards. He would typically put three or four microphones on the drums, and every instrumentalist would get a microphone as well. The background vocalists would share a microphone, while the lead singer would get Coxson's "top-of-the-line" Neumann U-67 microphone. The Wailers recorded a number of songs during those first sessions at Studio One, including "Simmer Down," "I'm Still Waiting," and "It Hurts to Be Alone." To Ranglin, some of the compositions felt unfinished. The Skatalites got right to work on shaping the Wailers' material. After the Skatalites hooked up their instruments, warmed up a bit, and worked out some arrangements, they recorded their first track with the group: "Simmer Down." Then they began to flesh out some of the Wailers' other material. " 'I'm Still Waiting' sounded good, y'know," Ranglin recalls. A few hours after the Wailers' first recording session, members of the group went to hear Coxson's sound system at a local dance. They were surprised to discover that Coxson was already playing "Simmer Down." It was cranked up loud, the sound echoing down the hallways of the Kingston night. In just a few hours, the group had gone from nobodies to hearing their voices booming across the sky. "Simmer down!" the crowd chanted along with the song. "Simmer down!" They demanded that the song be spun repeatedly. Friends waved at the Wailers from the dance floor and gave them friendly pats on the back. They had done it. People had laughed at them, and told them making a record was just a dream. People had advised them to find real jobs that made real money and promised a real future. They had endured sweaty practices in the afternoon sun and sleepy sessions in the wee hours of night. And now the band's song was actually getting played and people were actually dancing. "Simmer Down" was released as a single around Christmas of 1963. Coxson wanted the band to come back in and record more songs.

Great groups that last—U2, R.E.M., the Rolling Stones—are the exceptions. Many of the best bands in rock history were extremely short-lived. The Clash lasted only ten years. Rage Against the Machine endured for nine. The Police were around only eight. The Jam lasted seven. N.W.A broke up after five. Minor Threat ended after three. The Sex Pistols essentially released only one album before disintegrating. The qualities that make for great rock and roll (unpredictability, intensity, iconoclasm) contrast with the elements that make for enduring organizations (predictability, fraternity, trustworthiness). Tip the balance too far in one direction, and the band becomes a soulless musical mutual fund (the Eagles), go too far the other way and you wind up with a critically acclaimed corpse (Nirvana). Bruce Springsteen—who would share the bill with the Wailers for shows at Max's Kansas City in New York City in 1973—once said that "bands get formed by accident, but they don't survive by accident. It takes will, intent, a sense of shared purpose, and a tolerance for your friends' fallibilities—and they of yours. And that only evens the odds."

The Wailers ran into their first personnel problem soon after cutting their first records. Junior—who Coxson thought might have had the best voice in the group—was dropping out. His parents were leaving for America and Junior had to go with them. The other Wailers were shocked. Junior was one of the group's lead vocalists. He was a cornerstone of the group's harmonies. His singing blended particularly well with Beverly's, because they both had high-pitched voices. It was a terrible blow to the band. They had been living a dream. Now reality was catching up. Perhaps this was the way it would end. They would all be pulled away by practicality, torn from one another by work, family, money, life.

The remaining band members pulled together. There was plenty of camaraderie in the group at that time. There was much to be happy about. The Wailers had a hit song. "Simmer Down" would top the Jamaican single charts for several weeks. It would eventually sell more than seventy thousand copies. But there were a number of music stars living in Trench Town in those days. The Wailers were getting attention, but they were not overwhelmed. Still, the public interest made the members feel special. "I feel good! People used to call me 'Wailer!' as you walking on the street," Cherry said with a giggle. "You in the street and you hear 'Hey Wailer!' 'cause they didn't know my name. I didn't like it—but then I do." The Wailers had to walk through a cemetery to get to Studio One from Trench Town. The members would talk and sing most of the way. Sometimes Peter, Bunny, and Bob clowned around and pushed one another. Other times they pointed out people on the street and laughed about one thing or another. Cherry described her bandmates: "All of them were nice decent people. It was afterward that they got rough—especially Peter. Peter always joke around. Some people take it offensively, others take it for a joke."

In the studio, Bob was focused on his work. "He was shy and he was quiet. Because he's always thinking," Cherry said of him. "He just sit there thinking and he play the guitar and come up with something." Coxson gave Bob a book of guitar chords to help him with his training. "It's like you never can tell what might happen," Bob said. "It can work so sometimes the words come first and sometimes the music. Sometimes you get a song outside on the street. That sounds so funny because most songs I write, half the song will come to me on the street. It happens so quick, the best ones them leave. I never get a chance to write it down. Come again another day." He continued to work on his songcraft. His composition "Lonesome Feeling" became a hit for the group in 1965. He poured into the song his feelings of being alone, of alienation and abandonment. It was not so much a song about love as it was a song about sadness. "That was the first serious song I wrote. I took a long time to find the words to say what I wanted to say," Bob was quoted as saying.

Coxson regularly trotted out his recording acts at his sound-system performances. Dances would be held in places like Carnival Lawn on North Street, and members of the Wailers would appear and mime the words to their songs. Coxson decided it was time for the group to perform for real. He had been moving into sponsoring live concerts and he expected the Wailers would be a draw. The Palace in Kingston was chosen as the venue for the Wailers' first real live show. The bill included some of the hottest Jamaican acts of the day: Delroy Wilson, Jackie Opel, Higgs & Wilson, the Soulettes (featuring a young singer named Alpharita Anderson). The Skatalites and the Vikings served as backing bands for the other groups.

The crowd was hungry for entertainment. Audience members kept wandering backstage for a look at the various groups. They were impatient for the event to start. The Wailers passed the time sharpening their vocal harmonies. Their confidence level was high. The crowd began to chant for the show to begin. "Waaailers! Waaailers! Waaailers!" went the cry. The band members wondered if they could deliver. Yes, they were focused. Yes, they had put in the practice time. But the mob chanting for the Wailers had never even seen the Wailers before. They knew the band only from radio and records. What would they make of their live act? What if something went wrong? What if a mike went dead, or one of the group members tripped or some other of a million possible disasters? Still the chant went on: "Waaaaailers! Waaaaailers! Waaaaailers!" The promoters worried the crowd could get out of control. The curtain was raised forty-five minutes early.

The chant grew louder—"Waaaaaaaaaailers! Waaaaaaaaaailers! Waaaaaaaaaailers!"—as the group took the stage. Having a crowd chant your name in a daydream is fun. In real life, it's intimidating. You have to perform. You have to satisfy. And you are outnumbered. Bunny said the screams from the crowd were deafening. The group started by singing "Simmer Down." The audience reaction was so passionate the concert was nearly aborted right there. Boys pushed and elbowed one another, jockeying for places near the front. The Wailers then moved on to "I Don't Need Your Love" and a gospel song, "Amen." Girls, close to fainting, raised their arms and closed their eyes, as if they were testifying in church. The set was going along perfectly. With Junior gone, Bob took the lead on "It Hurts to Be Alone." This would be a major test. The crowd had heard the record. Would they like it live? Would they accept Bob's version? Or did the group die when Junior left? Bob had just started singing when the lights went out.

The whole island was experiencing an electrical blackout. But the audience had no idea what was going on. Many thought that they were being cheated out of the end of a great concert. They wanted to get the remaining portion of their money's worth. Fans began to hurl bottles and other debris at the stage. Things were going wild. Everything was in darkness. There were screams and the shattering sounds of broken glass. The members of the Wailers and the Soulettes locked themselves in a toilet together and waited for the rampage to die down. "It was frightening," Bunny says. "We stayed there until we were quite sure that everyone had left the theater." The experience inspired Bob to compose the song "Hooligan" and Peter to write the song "Jumbie Jamboree." Both became hits in 1965.

Other wild stage shows followed as the Wailers' singles shot up the charts. Something in the band's music connected. It made Jamaican kids stand up and do things. Seeing the Wailers onstage was like seeing themselves onstage. It made them realize that they had something to say and that what they were holding inside should come out. It made them dance, shout, even throw the most unexpected objects. At one performance at the Ward Theatre, Peter was struck in the head by a coin. And then hundreds of audience members followed suit, emptying their wallets and purses and hurling loose change. It was a surprising display of support, because Jamaican youth, in general, couldn't afford to throw away money. The hurled coins hurt when they hit—but they were not unwelcome. Peter stooped over and filled his pockets with change. Afterward, some audience members came backstage to ask for their change back. They had apparently just been caught up in the moment. Music, for a few spellbinding minutes, had become more important than money.

The rude-boy era had arrived. Jamaican youth were changing. For one, there were many more of them. In 1950, there were 1,403,000 people on the island; by 1957, there were 1,594,000—

a gain of one-seventh in seven years. It was a rate of growth that was higher than that of the world's total population over that period, and twice the rate of growth that prevailed in the middle of the nineteenth century. Those youths, born in the 1950s, were coming of age in the 1960s, looking for jobs and direction. In the mid-1960s in Jamaica, unemployment was up, hope was down. The number of people out of work exceeded 25 percent. The infant mortality rate at the close of the decade was three times that of Europe and America. Kids were being born faster and dying faster as well. Between 1950 and 1960, gross domestic product on the island had increased from 70 million pounds to 230 million pounds thanks in large part to the growth of the bauxite industry (which provided the raw material for aluminum). But the money from the boom bypassed the lower classes and went straight to the rich, resulting in even greater class tensions. The burst of optimism that followed independence had given way to grim reality. Young people were especially cynical about the future. The island of Jamaica is just 146 miles by 51 miles. In the cities on the coast, the water is rarely out of sight. It is easy to feel one's life and expectations have fixed boundaries. With so much water so close, it's easy to feel like you're always drowning.

Jamaica was an independent country. Now the children of Jamaica wanted to be independent, too. Many young people began calling themselves "rude boys." To be a rude boy was to be tougher than tough, to be an outsider, to be a rebel. Ska was the music of the rude boys and the Wailers were identified as part of the rude-boy world. Junior once boasted: "We were the voice of the rude boys." The band members began to feel that they were on a mission. It wasn't just about music anymore, it was about the kids on the street. It was about saying the things that weren't being said by teachers in school. Why were they being taught about British pirates and explorers and kings and queens? It was time to talk about what people their age were talking about. Music gave them an opportunity to do that. The Wailers would make music to wake a generation from their school-induced daze.

In 1962, the island had adopted a new national anthem, "Jamaica, Land We Love." The following year, the country's youth embraced an unofficial anthem: "Simmer Down." The Wailers songbook had become a hymnal for young people in Jamaica. The band's composition "Hooligan" was seen as the first true rude-boy song. Other Wailers songs that explored and explained the frustrations of Jamaican youth followed: "Rude Boy," a.k.a. "Rude Boy Ska," a.k.a. "Rule Them Rudie," and "Jailhouse," a.k.a. "Good God Rudie" and "Rudie Boy." These songs didn't criticize the youth, they glorified them. Young people who felt that they were being ostracized by society and locked out by the system found understanding and empathy in the music of the Wailers. "There was a lot of militant people who don't joke a lot," Bob pointed out. "Trench Town guerrillas. That helped the music. Them the people who used to dance to the music at that time. People called them rude boy. Anywhere the rude music played, that's where the people was. It helped to set a trend." When you can get guerrillas to dance, you know you've got something.

If you were in Lime Cay, Jamaica, on September 9, 1948, you would have witnessed a man being killed and a folk hero being born. On that date, a local gangster named Ivanhoe Martin, a.k.a. Rhygin, was shot dead by Jamaican authorities during a gun battle. Rhygin had been waiting to escape the island and flee to Cuba when his hiding place had been discovered. Bob would no doubt have heard of the case. Rhygin's name was on the lips of many rude boys. Rhygin murdered four policemen before he was slain. His life, and death, became a symbol of resistance and gangster style. He inspired the 1972 film *The Harder They Come*—the first feature film made and directed by a Jamaican and shot in Jamaica. A novel based on *The Harder They Come*, written by Michael Thelwell, was published in 1980 and dug even deeper into the Rhygin legend.

Little is known about Rhygin's actual motivations and life history. He may have been simply a murderous thug. The public, however, loves a good criminal. Jesse James, Bonnie and Clyde, John Gotti, and others have been celebrated for their felonious exploits. The criminal's reasons for his or her actions may be petty and mean. But the public often invents motivations for criminals that are grander and worthier of adulation. The breaking of rules becomes more important than the actual rules that are broken. Bob's lyrics were about challenging conventions and resisting the law. Rhygin fought the law, in all probability, for personal gain. Bob was driven by a larger purpose. He embraced the insurgent spirit that the public only imagined that Rhygin might have had.

In his early work, Bob would sing of "Burnin' and Lootin'." He would declare that "I Shot the Sheriff." He would sing of escaping jail cells, confronting authority, and running up against police roadblocks. Peter once toted a guitar shaped like an M-16. It was a fitting symbol for the Wailers' mission. Music was their weapon. Lyrics were their bullets. The Wailers took the lure of violence that drew the public to characters like Rhygin and transformed it into meaningful music. They took the urban rage that would inspire the genre of gangsta rap and harnessed it to serve humanistic goals. Rappers caught up in controversies over the content of their music often argue that they are simply reflecting reality. They say they are keeping it real. But keeping it real isn't enough when reality needs changing. The Wailers demonstrated that artists could both reflect reality and shape it to their will. True artists don't just hold up mirrors, they paint canvases.

There is a term in the gangsta-rap world to describe the founding fathers in the field: O.G. It stands for original gangsta. Bob was an O.G. He did not rap, he did not break-dance, and he wasn't known for spraying graffiti tags on Kingston buildings. But his music was composed of songs from the streets. He was born, as an artist, in the same cultural mix that gave birth to hip-hop. The producers he worked with in Jamaica invented some of the techniques that would later be employed by rap producers in America. Bob began his career as a vocalist, but he was, at his heart, a storyteller. His song "Johnny Was" tells the tale of a good man gunned down at an early age. His song "War" is a kind of proto-rap, setting a speech by Haile Selassie to music. The focus is on the words, not the melody. Marley was not drawn to duets in his lifetime, but after his death, scores of rappers recorded posthumous rap-reggae duets with Marley. Lauryn Hill recorded a version of "Turn Your Lights Down Low" (she also sampled "Concrete Jungle" on her Grammy-winning debut album and gave birth to several Marley grandchildren). Producers intertwined Bob's voice with the Notorious B.I.G.'s to create a new track, years after both performers had passed. Other rappers, including Eve and Queen Latifah, have recorded versions of his songs. Dance-hall artists cite Bob as an inspiration, even as they stray from his life-affirming message.

Bob's connection to the rap world is an important one. It helps to show that reggae was bigger than reggae. Jamaica is an island, but its culture conquered continents. Marley struggled in vain to make inroads with black American music fans. In death, he launched a new career as a hip-hop icon. America rejected him in life but embraced him in the grave.

Like other Jamaican youths in the 1960s, the Wailers found themselves harassed by police. The experiences hardened their outlook. Bob observed: "We were well trained. During my time growing up in Jamaica, from when I reach sixteen, seventeen, from when I reach eighteen, I never stop running from the police." The Wailers' rehearsals took on an increased sense of urgency. Music seemed the only route to safety. Said Bunny: "The thing about the Wailers is we rehearsed a lot. And we always tried to get ourselves prepared so when the time came to be recorded we knew exactly what we wanted. In those days you didn't have a lot of money to throw away on records. Every song had its price. So we had to as best we could come up with the kind of arrangement that make everything sound different. That makes every song sound different from every song."

The practice sessions were tough on the members, especially Beverly and Cherry. Bob would demand that songs be performed repeatedly. He wanted the music to match the perfection he heard in his head. "I stopped singin' because of Bob's attitude about the music," Beverly complained. "We would be practicing a song like 'Lonesome Feelings' or 'It Hurts to Be Alone'—so many songs I can't remember them all—and if you make a mistake he would jump down on you and be very tough, because that's the way he was taught. But I was too quiet and shy, and I'd start crying and say, 'Oh, I'm gonna leave.' "

Bob would sometimes go up to her and apologize.

"Oh, Beverly, you know how I am," Bob said.

Beverly was also troubled by the fact that members of the group had started smoking ganja. Studio One was soundproof and almost airtight. She wasn't a smoker and the druggy haze made her choke and gasp for breath. Jokes would be told and she wouldn't get them. Maybe they weren't really jokes at all, but because everyone was high, everyone laughed. Beverly felt isolated. She was in a group and she felt alone. It just wasn't fun anymore. The male band members told her that the real problem wasn't that they were smoking, it was that Beverly needed to take up the practice.

Cherry was the first female member to exit the band. The band wasn't started just for kicks—it was founded to make money. The Wailers were making hit records, but they weren't seeing any returns. To Cherry, it just wasn't worth it. She had a child to take care of, and needed to focus on making a steady income. Cherry says she can recall getting paid only once for her work by Coxson: "He gave us five pounds one day. We recorded 'Maga Dog' [a song written by Peter Tosh] and we was having a concert, and he gave me five pounds and he gave Beverly five pounds to buy a dress. And we buy the materials, 'cause I used to sew. And I made my dress and Beverly's sister made hers."

After Cherry's departure, Beverly announced she was leaving. Bunny, Bob, and Peter thought this was bad news for the group. They decided they would fight to keep her. They even composed a new song, "Donna," to lure her back into the fold. It didn't work. Beverly left the band in 1966. The Wailers were falling apart.

The Wailers were having trouble staying together because they weren't making enough money as a band. They would eventually record more than one hundred singles for Coxson and generate dozens of hit records. Coxson had them record a bewildering range of songs, including Tom Jones's "What's New, Pussycat?," the Beatles' "And I Love Her," and even a version of "White Christmas." The Wailers maintained a grueling appearance and concert schedule. In April 1965, they played three shows a day as part of the "Oriental Playgirls and Sepia Revue," which was billed as "a fabulous package of oriental beauty and talent integrated with your favourite coloured recording stars." As part of the gig, the band performed songs as three international beauty queens walked the stage: "Miss Tokyo, Miss Hong Kong, Miss United Nations." At another appearance in June 1965, at the Regal Theatre, the Wailers were part of "Battle of the Greats: Ska vs. Jazz," in which they faced off in a battle of the bands with jazz acts.

The Wailers were winning battles, but losing themselves.

Bob's mother had moved to Delaware around the time he began recording, so he was essentially homeless. He started sleeping in the back of Studio One. All the members of the group were short on money and resources. One day at rehearsal, Bunny went out and bought a bulla—a sweet cake made out of sugar and flour. There was enough money for only one bulla, so the whole band had to share, one bite each. The Wailers were stars on the radio, but in real life their stomachs were growling. "Everything happened so fast that our fans and the record-buying public did not realize what the situation was with the Wailers," Bunny grumbles. "That although we were hitting the charts, and selling a lot of records and creating preposterous returns, the Wailers inherited very little compared to Coxson and many other personnel, companies, organizations, and industry on the whole. With a salary of three pounds per week and no form of royalty whatsoever, Coxson made the Wailers hungry and frustrated."

The Wailers had started as a larger group because there were five members in successful groups such as the Platters, the Imperials, and the Drifters. Pared down to a trio, the members of the band began to do some research into three-man outfits. Coxson allowed them to listen to some of the songs in his music library. One of Bob's jobs at Studio One was to listen to all the records Coxson was sent from all around the world to play on his sound system. The records were piled up on a table that also served as Bob's bed. Before he went to sleep at night, he would first have to listen to dozens of them. The other Wailers also listened to some of these releases. They checked out groups and solo acts, looking for sounds to emulate. They played records by James Brown, Wilson Pickett, Ray Charles, Fats Domino, Louis Prima, the Coasters, Clyde McPhatter, Louis Armstrong, Joe Tex, and Percy Sledge. The group that seemed to stand out was the Impressions. The Impressions seemed to be like the Wailers. "Those songs was strictly rhythm-and-blues influence, y'know, because rhythm and blues was strong influence down in Jamaica during those times," Bob said about the Wailers' recordings with Coxson. "Those type of music was influence down there at the time was Curtis Mayfield and the Impressions." The Impressions wrote their own songs and seemed to believe in their own singing and composing abilities, and that appealed to the Wailers. Said Bunny: "Guided by the technique of the Impressions, we developed a style comparable, but completely different."

But the new trio was about to lose its most important member.

BABY WE'VE GOT A DATE
(ROCK IT BABY)

The Wailers were adored by girls all over Jamaica. But during the early years of the band's existence, dating was not the Wailers' primary concern. They were fixed on their careers. They had all worked too hard to get distracted. "Girls are hungry and need food," Bunny grouses. "Girls have babies and need fathers. We were focused on the people's well-being and welfare and what was happening to us as part of the people and the environment that we grew up in. That's what made the Wailers, that's what drew the attention of the world to the Wailers—not girls . . . We were a bunch of guys in a profession, looking for a way to make money. We were obligated to do so. We were really focused on music professionally, and getting our career really out there in the world so we could take care of all our little problems and endeavors and stuff like that. So we weren't going after girls. Girls came in later on."

But there was one woman who caught Bob's eye. Her name was Alpharita Constantia Anderson. Friends called her Rita. People who thought little of her did so at their peril. Rita was as determined as an anthill. She would appear, at first, as a tiny little worker and then swarm the obstacles in her way. Rita's mother was Cuban; although numerous sources say Rita was also born in Cuba, she insists she is a native of Kingston. She lived in the same area of Trench Town as the Wailers. They would pass by her house on the way to Studio One. Rita would stand at her gate. Her baby, Sharon, would be in her arms. Rita would wave to the Wailers. Sometimes the guys in the group would laugh. Why was she waving? Beverly would lag behind and play with Rita's baby. Rita and Beverly would talk. Rita was a fan of the Wailers. She especially liked their song "Lonesome Feeling." She was studying to become a nurse at the Bethesda School of Practical Nursing and was enrolled in night school to learn shorthand and typing. But she wanted to give singing a try. Beverly told her to come in and see Coxson for an audition. Rita was quickly signed to become part of a new group, the Soulettes, with Marlene "Precious" Gifford (a girlfriend of Rita's) and Constantine "Dream" Walker (Rita's cousin). Bob was put in charge of writing and arranging songs for the group.

Rita found Bob to be a serious young man. When he was working he was stern. He didn't laugh. He wasn't looking to have fun. He was focused on getting out of the gutter. Rita felt they had a similar outlook on life. She was also determined to better her situation. Rita, at first, didn't have romance on her mind. "I was thinking about music," she says, and laughs. "It was about music at that stage. Because I already had a baby, Sharon, so I really wasn't looking for a boyfriend, y'know. I had a boyfriend. So I was looking for the music in him, because I heard about the Wailers." Bob quickly charmed her. He took Rita out on a date to the Ambassador. It was a theater in Trench Town that held concerts and showed movies. During the movie, they shared their first kiss. Bob and Rita soon began a relationship. Not long afterward, Rita told Bob she was pregnant with his child.

Sex in Jamaica was poisoned by slavery. Marriage was prohibited between slaves by law. Promiscuity among slaves was encouraged by masters, who believed that if slave women had multiple partners, they would be more likely to breed. During the eighteenth century, there were very few white women in Jamaica, so white masters frequently raped their black female slaves. The result was a large mixed-race population. Light skin became valued; dark skin, devalued. Throughout the nineteenth and twentieth centuries, bleaching creams became popular on the island. The products often scarred and spotted users.

There was plenty of sex being had in Jamaica, but in the 1960s, it wasn't talked about openly. (Things may not have changed much since.) In 1961, a study found that almost half of Jamaican men said they had lost their virginity before the age of thirteen. The men may have been boasting, but the results were still telling. Pro-fertility values were common in Jamaica. In some country parishes, a girl who hadn't produced a baby by age fifteen was called a mule. There was also once a widespread belief that a woman had a preordained lot of babies. If she didn't fill her quota, she would fall ill. Two-thirds of Jamaican women have sex within four years of their first menstruation. In the 1960s, many young people on the island had not heard of contraception, or believed it to be a dangerous practice. There was talk that condoms would "fly up into the shoulder." Another tale had it that an IUD would "suck you down." Only 6 percent of Jamaican women had ever tried contraception before their first pregnancy. Very few parents talked to their kids about the facts of life. Girls were often told simply to stay away from boys. A common tale that was told to girls was that babies were "vomited up" through the mouth. With all the misinformation, many young Jamaicans were foregoing marriage and stable relationships. Out-of-wedlock babies were common. Men with babies by several different women were common as well. Around the time Bob and Rita became engaged, only 10.2 percent of the women in Kingston Parish between the ages of fourteen and forty-four were legally married.

Bob would have plenty of lovers over his short life. But, in his own mind, he felt he showed women great respect. Once, when asked by reporters if women were "oppressed," Bob answered, "Of course." When asked if women were mentally different from men, Bob replied: "No, I don't think there is anything different up there." He did feel women "approached things different" from men. "Let me tell you—I wouldn't send no woman to put a truck engine in a truck," Bob once pronounced. "But woman must be respected and cared for and treated right." Another time, when asked about Black Power activist Angela Davis, Marley answered, "Dat woman in America . . . Angela Davis, a woman like that who defends something: Me can appreciate that." Later in life, when he embraced Rastafari, he grew frustrated at the idea advanced by some reporters that the new faith was sexist. "Let me tell you, them spread this propaganda so that the woman might have a bad feeling toward Rasta without even knowing," Bob vented. "But all of that . . . we call it propaganda. It's not true. Women is our mudder." He felt a special sense of obligation toward Rita. For her part, she couldn't stop his infidelities, so she tried to put them out of her mind. Rita confessed: "I was never mingled in the other women's affairs. I was always his very special one. When God put you together, you remain together no matter what happens."

Bob wanted to support Rita properly. The Wailers were popular, but they were broke. All the Wailers felt frustrated and angry about the way the music industry had treated them. "Them only hear the cash register," Bob accused. There seemed to be no way for artists to profit from their talent and hard work. Bob's list of complaints continued: "Them guys on the machine [the producers] all them wanna do is hustle quick—like you find a guy put out two hundred songs a year with sixty different labels and nine hundred different singers. And like them guys don't play no music, them only have the equipment, and them try and make it so you don't get no money."

Bob decided to follow a long-standing tradition of young men looking to make it in Jamaica—they go to America. He made plans to travel to Wilmington, Delaware, and live with his mother. Cedella and Bunny's father had broken up. She had recently married an American man and wanted Bob to join her in the States. Bob figured that in America he would be able to earn enough money to support his new family. "His mother sent for him," recounts Rita. "That was her plan from the initial stage. Go to America, get married to an American, and then she would sponsor her children. She had that in mind, that was the plan, she promised him that, that when I go to America, I will send for you."

On February 10, 1966, at 11 A.M., Bob and Rita were married. The ceremony took place in the office of the justice of the peace. Rita wore a white ruffled wedding dress with long lace sleeves and a borrowed mother-of-pearl tiara. She was nineteen, and Bob had just turned twenty-one. Rita's first child, Sharon, was almost a year old. Bunny said it was "a wedding to which Peter and I were never invited or even were aware of. Strange, isn't it?" Rita said the ceremony took her and Bob by surprise. She confided: "I didn't plan to get married, we didn't plan to get married. When he realize that his mother had gotten through with his papers, then she said to him, 'Okay, it's time to come, your papers are ready, your sponsorship papers are ready and you have to come right tomorrow.' And then he said he didn't want to leave me, we were really getting deeper in love, and he said he wouldn't leave me and so he asked my aunt if she would allow me to marry to him. Y'know, because I was living with my auntie, she was my mommy."

A few days after the wedding, Bob left for America. Just as his father had done, he left a young mother behind in order to pursue business affairs somewhere far away.

Bob would journey to Delaware to fund his dreams. Rita would pay the price for it. Great artists are often driven by the opposite sex. The Greeks believed that inspiration came from the Muses, divine women who were the daughters of Zeus. In real life, throughout the centuries, many of the greatest poets, painters, novelists, and musicians have employed human muses. Dante had his Beatrice (a Florentine beauty he was obsessed with his whole life). Rodin's most productive period was the fifteen-year span in which Camille Claudel served as his studio assistant and lover. The critic Denis Donoghue observed that T. S. Eliot's most famous poem, *The Waste Land*, "issued, however circuitously, from the unhappiness of Eliot's first marriage [to Vivienne Eliot]." Vladimir Nabokov's spouse, Vera, contributed to the writing of *Speak, Memory* and prevented him from incinerating early drafts of *Lolita*. "Without my wife, I wouldn't have written a single novel," Nabokov confessed. F. Scott Fitzgerald incorporated conversations with his wife, Zelda, passages from her fiction, and even lines from her letters into his own work, leading Zelda to quip: "Plagiarism begins at home."

Was Rita a muse or a meddler? The former is certainly the case. Rita is intimately intertwined with Bob's greatness. Many of his finest songs, including "Nice Time," "Chances Are," and "No Woman, No Cry," were inspired by their personal life. Rita was also his primary backing vocalist and was officially credited with writing several of his songs, including the title track for his first solo album, *Natty Dread*. She sang backup on every one of his major-label albums. She was a muse to him in every sense that matters.

A true muse is more than a wife, more than a lover or longtime companion, more than a sounding board for ideas and intentions. A true muse is integral to the artistic process; a true muse, to use Dante's description of Beatrice, is a "bringer of blessings"—a catalyst for, conduit to, and conjurer of an artist's best and truest aesthetic self. A muse may offer rivalry, argument, and informed feedback; a muse may offer consolation and comfort in the form of kind words or fiery lovemaking. Whatever the particulars of each muse-artist relationship, this much is true: artists—not all perhaps, but many of the greatest—need muses, whether real or imagined. No matter how immense their skill, no matter how established their reputations, that moment of inspiration, that tender time when true breakthrough thoughts and ideas come crashing or slipping or striding into the consciousness, often remains mysterious even to those who experience it. "[The artist's] truth does not belong to the realm of the demonstrable; it is a matter of faith," French author André Malraux once wrote. "If asked 'Why do you paint this way?' he can only answer, 'Because it is the right way.' " Baffled by their own genius, blind to the source of their own vision, artists often require muses to bring them the present of their own best selves.

According to Rita, Bob often turned to her for artistic guidance. He might call her up and ask, "Did you read what I did last night—it's on the table." He would ask her about a lyric or a particular sound in a song to get her reaction. She claims that many of Bob's lyrics came from the life they shared and that they did a lot of writing as a team. Sometimes they both went through the Bible together, searching for guidance.

Not all masterpieces, of course, are inspired by muses, but a surprising and significant number have been. Nora Joyce, wife of James Joyce, was the model for Molly Bloom in *Ulysses*. Flaubert drew on his relationship with his muse, the poet/journalist/playwright Louise Colet, to write his masterpiece, *Madame Bovary*. Artists seem to find in the heat of passion the power to manufacture new ideas, to fuse together disparate elements of thought; accordingly, muses are often wild, sexual beings who unleash an artist's creative energy by unlocking his inhibitions. Nora and James Joyce exchanged a series of sexually explicit, taboo-breaking letters in which he begged her to "write more and dirtier, darling." Rita says she was the inspiration for the food and sex metaphors in Bob's classic song "Stir It Up."

The story of Rita and Bob is the untold story of how art actually comes into being out of confusion, tension, exertion, imagination, passion—and collaboration. There is a revelatory power that some artists see in certain people which gives them access to a kind of grace and enchantment that they cannot achieve alone. It is an energy that liberates the imagination even as it sometimes enslaves the heart. Dante recorded his first meeting with Beatrice with this passage: "The least pulse of my body shook therewith; and in trembling it said these words: 'Here is a deity stronger than I, who, coming, shall rule over me.'" And James Joyce once wrote Nora the following letter: "You have me completely in your power. I know and I feel that if I am to write anything fine and noble in the future I shall do so only by listening at the doors of your heart." Bob would often whisper "I love you" into Rita's ear while they were onstage. He would send her letters from Delaware pledging his devotion. These words, of course, could be examples of artists, like any frail humans, caught up in the love-drunk hyperbole of romance. But they are likely something more sig-

nificant; Dante and Joyce were not known for using words indis-
criminately and unwisely. Neither was Bob. He never divorced
Rita and never married another woman.

But Bob and Rita did have a rocky relationship. Artists, searching out new ideas and new ways of looking at the world, often
seek out emotional and experiential extremes, in the form of sui-
cidal behavior, wild arguments, multiple sex partners, drugs, and
alcohol. Carl Jung once observed that "the artist's life cannot be
otherwise than full of conflicts, for two forces are at war within
him—on the one hand the common human longing for happiness,
satisfaction and security in life, and on the other a ruthless passion
for creation which may go so far as to override every personal
desire . . . There are hardly any exceptions to the rule that a person must pay dearly for the divine gift of the creative fire."

As a listener, your relationship with a band is like a love affair.
You hear that first single on the radio and it's like eyes meeting
across the room. You buy the single, or the album, and it's a first
date. You play the album several times, and go to the store to
purchase more recordings by the same group. You're going steady
now, and you're spending more time together. Finally, it's time to
get serious. It's time for commitment. You decide to go all the
way. You see the band in concert. It's dark and it's sweaty. You're
a bit nervous, because maybe it's your first time. Things are awkward at first, and there is shouting and moaning and limbs everywhere. Everything builds to a climax. When it's over, you're
exhausted but satisfied. You want to be with this band for the rest
of your life.

The average rock fan is a jealous lover. They want the band they
adore all to themselves. Most rock bands are male, so it is female
companions who have taken the brunt of fan criticism. Over the

years, an evil triumvirate has been formed. A trio of rock-and-roll devil women who dared to come between fans and their bands: Yoko Ono and the Beatles, Courtney Love and Nirvana, Rita and the Wailers. The fans charge them with being talentless. They suspect them of being gold diggers. They accuse them of the highest crime in pop music: breaking up a great band.

Ono, Love, and Rita have something else in common. Each is an abundantly talented artist who settled for being a muse. Because of this choice, their motives have been misunderstood, their artistic abilities slighted, and they have been demonized by the public. Peter and Bunny never got around to completely trusting Rita. "She was a Wailer's wife and we respected her as our sister," Bunny once declared. "But were we her brothers?"

Ono was much more than a distraction for the Beatles. Ono and John Lennon shared a close working relationship, collaborating on political actions, art installments, and musical compositions. Ono often took the lead role in dealing with the outside world. "In a relationship I think women really have sort of the wisdom to cope with society since they created it," Ono observed. "Men never developed the inner wisdom; they didn't have time. So most men do rely on women's inner wisdom, whether they express that or not." Lennon, although an established rock star as a member of the Beatles long before he met Ono, nonetheless attributed much of his success to his wife: "It is a teacher-pupil relationship. That's what people don't understand. She's the teacher and I'm the pupil. I'm the famous one, the one who's supposed to know everything, but she's my teacher. She's taught me everything I . . . know. She was there when I was the nowhere man."

Courtney Love was much more than rock star Kurt Cobain's junkie lover. When they met, she was the front woman for the art-punk band Hole, a group that at one point had nearly as much buzz as Nirvana. Hole's best album, *Live Through This*, received as much critical adulation as almost any album released in the heyday of alternative rock. And there's little question Love and Cobain shared sexual passion. Cobain once proudly displayed the raw, red nail marks that his rock-star wife, Courtney Love, ripped down his back during their lovemaking.

Why do strong women consent to standing in the shadows of great male artists? In some cases, singing a duet of sorts is the only way that a female artist's voice will be heard. Over the years, the artistic abilities of women have been disparaged by some of the greatest male intellectuals and critics. "Instead of calling them beautiful, there would be more warrant for describing women as the unaesthetic sex. Neither for music, nor for poetry, nor for fine art, have they really and truly any sense or susceptibility," said Arthur Schopenhauer in 1851. When *Rolling Stone* compiled a list of the hundred greatest guitarists in rock, only two women made the list, Joan Jett and Joni Mitchell.

Whitney Chadwick, in her book *Women, Art and Society*, relates a striking anecdote. In the 1700s, academies ruled the art world, and an artist had to be a member in order to receive recognition and commissions. Two of the founding members of the British Royal Academy in 1768 were female painters, Angelica Kauffmann and Mary Moser. However, when Johann Zoffany painted a portrait of the members, *The Academicians of the Royal Academy* (1771–72), a formal picture that showed a cluster of male artists studying several seminude male models, the two founding women were not included in the group. Instead, the faces of the two women were depicted on the fringes of the portrait, as busts mounted on a wall—paintings within a painting. They had been reduced from artists to objects.

Ono, Love, and Rita have all been portrayed, at one time or another, as scheming, deceitful, possibly even crazy. But to women with the creative fire burning within them, being an object of some other artist's art, relegating one's self to inspiring another's act of creation, could provoke frustration, rage, and even a wild state of mind that society would all too often label madness. Zelda Fitzgerald, as well as Vivienne Eliot and Camille Claudel—all muses, all underappreciated artists—were eventually committed to mental institutions. In *The Female Malady: Women, Madness, and English Culture, 1830–1980*, Elaine Showalter argues that such "mental breakdowns" are the result of cultures that deprive women of "social or intellectual outlets or expressive options" and the right "to speak and act . . . in the public world." On March 3, 1930, Camille sent her brother, Paul, this letter from the asylum to which she had been committed: "Don't forget that Rodin's wife was an old model of his: now do you see the scheme of which I was the object? It's nice, all these millionaires who attack a poor defenseless artist! . . . That is exploiting women, crushing the artist who is made to sweat blood!"

Rita Marley would feel some of the same rage.

Cedella and her new American husband, Edward Booker, picked Bob up at the airport in Philadelphia and drove him to Wilmington. There is no snow in Jamaica, except on the tops of some mountains. Bob had never experienced cold like Delaware's deep freeze. American culture and the climate left him with a chill. Bob and Rita wrote letters back and forth about what they were going through. "We did a lot of correspondence, man, it was very painful for him, more so than me, because he went into a different environment for the first time," Rita remembers. "And it was wintertime when he went to Delaware. You know Delaware, when it's winter there, it's like a freezer, you don't want to stay outside. So all of that was like, 'Why did I come here? Why did you not tell me not to come?' "

Bob felt out of place in Delaware. He was a black man in a

white state. He liked it warm, and the weather was cold. He missed the palm trees and the doctor birds, the warm streams and the sweet fruits. He also missed his friends. He had dreamed of leaving Trench Town. He realized how connected he was to the place. Said Bob: "When you grow up with a lot of people who you know and all upon a sudden you don't see them again, [is] dangerous feeling, mon. You miss all the likkle tracks you used to walk. So, bwoy, you know that you never ever going to get anything like that around this, 'caw is a different thing here."

Rita, for her part, missed her husband. She was a newlywed with an empty bed. She already had one daughter to care for. And now she was pregnant with Bob's first child with her, Cedella. She was beginning a family, but she was doing it all alone. "I was frightened, for truth," Rita admits. "Because I didn't know this was what marriage was all about. So I was very frightened, very scared, in terms of what do I do now? But then we would write letters like every day. Every day, letters would be going and coming. And Peter and Bunny would sort of encourage me to still keep singing, to come to the studio and still sing with them, but Bob didn't want me to do that, he said I should stay home and read my Bible."

Bob would later tell reporters that he lived in Wilmington for nine months in 1966. "Me stay in America one time for nine months but it was a big experience," he said. Another time he joked: "Yes mon! During that time, nine months was the longest nine months I ever spent." He would say his job was "working at Chrysler, in a place called Newark [in Delaware]. Spare parts section." But he spent much longer than nine months in Delaware and he had several jobs. He first moved there in 1966 and lived with his mother and his half sister Pearl at 2313 Tatnall Street. Although he did return to Jamaica in late 1966, he maintained roots in Delaware for years afterward, returning there on occasion to earn extra money. Sometime between 1966 and 1969, he was joined by Rita and he moved next door to his mother, at 2311 Tatnall Street. Bob held a series of odd jobs, working at a Du Pont Chemical factory, sweeping up at a hotel, and working at the Chrysler automotive assembly plant in Newark, Delaware.

Rita says Bob had a strong work ethic, whether he was onstage or on the assembly line. "Chrysler. He got a job at Chrysler. Poor Bob. He's not a lazy guy. That is to show you how ambitious this young man was. He kept trying because he got married at an early age when all his friends said, 'Are you crazy, what you getting married for at this age?' 'Young bwoy, you gotta a life to live, plenty girls out there,' and things like that. But then Bob took his life, his whole family relationship, was serious to him, most important. So he felt he had to find jobs to send money for Rita, and to children, they have to school, and Rita has to get this, and they want to leave Trench Town. So he was carrying his responsibility like a man. When everyone else was acting like a boy, Bob would be like a man. Y'know? That was one of the things that I admired in him—he held responsibility. I would feel comfortable saying that's my man, because he treats me like a lady, and he know how to keep a house—y'know like bring home the food, bring home the milk for the baby, see something nice and bring it for the baby—see, I bring an apple for you or a few grapes? He never come home one evening empty-handed and that was a good sign. If it's even three oranges. He was a special guy."

Rita and Bob and their children lived together in Delaware in the early 1970s. He would travel back and forth between Jamaica and America. Their family began to grow. There was Sharon (born in 1965, she was Rita's daughter but Bob adopted her as his own), Cedella (born 1967 in Jamaica), Ziggy (born 1968 in Jamaica), and Stephen (born 1972 in Wilmington, Delaware). Cedella recalls her father heading off to work each day to go to "the plant."

For the children, the times were tough. Remarks Cedella: "It was hard for us as children to come here. Black Jamaicans versus black Americans, the kids were kind of mean. They didn't understand the way we spoke—and we did it on purpose, too. My great-aunt came to live with us, too, in Delaware. We had to bring her down to the school one day to take on this bully who wouldn't leave us alone—and he thought she was like some sort of witch because she spoke heavy Jamaican patois. She scared him off."

Cedella says Bob was a gentle parent. "He wasn't a disciplinarian." She laughs. "That was Mom's job. He kind of chickened out on that. Whenever she disciplined us—you have one parent who does the makeup, so after we would get like spanked or talked to, all it took was a word and we'd start crying and he would be the one to take us for ice cream."

Marley was still working at Chrysler in 1968. He was a card-carrying member of the United Auto Workers union. He had a job at the Chrysler Newark Assembly Plant in Newark, Delaware, on South College Avenue. The plant employed about two thousand people. Half worked the first shift, 5:30 A.M. to 2:48 P.M.; the other half worked second shift, 3:30 P.M. to 12:30 A.M. Bob usually worked second shift. The experience would later inspire his song "Nightshift." Bob didn't stand out much. He would punch in to the time clock at the start of his workday and punch out at the end. Like other employees, he dressed casually, in jeans and a work shirt. His hair was short and without dreadlocks. He would usually wear a brimless cap in the Rasta colors of red, gold, and green.

Bob worked in the body shop. He drove a forklift and transported materials to workers on the assembly lines. They were mostly building family cars—station wagons, sedans, etc. The lines Bob supplied put on fenders, back doors, and other parts of the back sections of vehicles. When someone on the line ran out of materials, Bob would take away their empty case and return with a new case of fresh materials.

Bob had a half hour for lunch. There were two cafeterias in the plant, but he usually ate where he worked, sitting in the stacks with spare car parts all around him. Sometimes, during breaks, he played a spirited game of dominoes with some of the other workers in his area. When he did go down to the cafeteria, other workers sometimes gathered around him. Bob wasn't flashy, but other employees were drawn to the way he spoke. They were intrigued by the Jamaican lilt in his voice and his passion. He often talked about music. He told people that he had a band. Some believed him; most didn't. Said Hilton Snead, who was an employee at Chrysler at the time: "I think he was working to provide for his family. To survive and get the bills paid. I never heard him say he was saving money to promote his career."

One topic that often came up in conversations with Bob was race relations. It was the era of civil-rights struggles. The year before, Stokely Carmichael, a leader of the Student Nonviolent Coordinating Committee, had popularized the term *black power*. On April 4 of that year, Martin Luther King had been assassinated in Memphis, sparking race riots around the country. At the plant, racial tensions were high. "It was not wide open," said Snead. "It was a little bit undercover. We had to work together, blacks and whites, to do what we had to do—building cars." Still, there were plenty of suspicions and accusations when blacks were passed over for promotions. And there was much angry talk among black workers about the lack of black representation in the positions of influence in United Auto Workers Local 1183. Bob seemed interested in those discussions, but sometime late in 1968, he left his job at the plant.

While he was in Delaware Bob listened to American music. "Yeah, music all the while. Them time there," he said. "Marvin Gaye just come with some music and some other people. Stevie Wonder and them." He continued to write music as well. "Yeah, while I was there during that time, I was really inna me basement, work out some stuff," he recounted. "Write couple songs, too, during that time and reach back in Jamaica and record them." Rita recalls: "He kept writing, yes, because sometimes in the letter he would say, tell me if you like this verse, and it would be a verse of something he wrote the night before. He never put his guitar down, y'know. And that is why his music is able to live after him."

Ibis Pitts operated Ibis Specialty and Gift Shop on Twenty-fourth and Market in Wilmington. He sold jewelry, tapestries, and African-style clothing and would often play jazz and African music on his stereo. During the summer of 1969, a shoeless woman in a black shirt came into his shop. The woman began dancing. It was Rita Marley. "She seemed so happy and she was barefoot," Pitts remembers. "You didn't usually see grown women in a store in downtown barefoot. So I asked her where she was from and she said Jamaica. She went on to say that she and her husband recorded a little something. The little record they gave me was 'Nice Time.' I used to play that little record over and over. I thought it was so beautiful, the sound and the music was so nice."

Later, Bob came down to the shop and he and Pitts became friends. Pitts would go over to Bob's mother's house and play music with him in the basement. Pitts played congas and Bob played guitar and sang. Pitts recalls one of the songs Bob was working on at the time was "Is This Love?" Bob also showed Pitts how he was growing an eight-foot-tall herb marijuana bush behind his mother's house.

Pitts had been planning to go to Woodstock that summer and he begged Bob to go with him. "Since he was an aspiring musician, I would think he'd want to go there," Pitts speculates. "Maybe he wasn't aware of who was going to be there—because I don't think I really was. I just knew it was a big festival and there was going to be good musicians there. I didn't know it was going to be like it was; it blew my mind." Bob, however, skipped the concert and stayed home.

Marley was mostly cut off from the music business and from the Wailers when he was in Delaware. Bunny and Peter had recruited Vision from the Soulettes to take Bob's place in the group. He had practiced with the Wailers in the past, so he was familiar with their songs and vocal approach. But still, to Bunny, it felt as if the band were starting all over again. Bunny, Peter, and Vision tried to press on with the group. According to Bunny's way of thinking: "It would have been a total loss to us, to the people that believed in us, to Jamaica, its music, and culture, the many artists . . . if we had discontinued our mission." The Wailers continued, recording such songs as "Who Feels It Knows It," "Dreamland," "The Toughest," "Sunday Morning," "Jerk in Time," and even a cover of Bob Dylan's "Like a Rolling Stone." "There was no alternative for the Wailers to take other than to get up and move on or ever be remembered for what we had already done, and without anything to show for what was done," Bunny reasoned.

But the Wailers were still broke, despite the new round of recordings. They tried to squeeze more money out of Coxson, but were rebuffed. Bunny began to see him more as a pharaoh than a producer. The Wailers turned to odd jobs to pay their bills. They did some arranging for other Studio One performers. They also began to audition newcomers to earn extra cash. They tried to stretch the nine pounds a week they got from Coxson as far as they could. But things were only getting harder. According to Bunny, the Wailers had to split the nine pounds four ways, since they felt it was only fair that Rita got Bob's weekly share.

Finally, Bunny and Peter had had enough of Coxson. They decided to take action. Bunny fumes: "I was now getting disgusted and fed up with Coxson's dirty system and I was prepared to go to war using the muscles that were available to us. Because we were the idols of the rude boys, Coxson Jackson and I had several verbal clashes, but he was careful enough not to get physical, as was his attitude whenever anyone pressured him for the justice due to them . . . In defense of our integrity, we decided to cease from doing any further recordings."

The Wailers had been with Coxson for several years. They had devoted fans all over Jamaica. Their fans imagined the Wailers to be rich and successful. It was galling to Bunny that this was far from the case. The Wailers were in the same economic state as the people who came to their concerts, perhaps even a bit worse. "Coxson deliberately programmed us this way so as to make us handicapped and helpless of even trying to do a recording of our own," Bunny charges. While Bob was in America Bunny didn't write to tell him what was happening with the Wailers. He thought the best way to encourage Bob to return was to refrain from corresponding with him. Bunny hoped the Wailers' fans would stay with the band until Bob came back to Kingston.

At some point in his stay in Delaware, Bob may have gotten a notice from the local draft board. The Vietnam War was ongoing and many young men were being called up. "Yes—that's one of the things that pulled him back home to Jamaica," Rita declares. "He was drafted and he said no way, no way, these guys want me to go and fight in the war. They wanted him to go to Vietnam, it was Vietnam happening in those days. And so he said no. Yeah, I got that letter and I didn't know what that meant. So I said to fight war, what's that?" Then again, Bob may have simply wanted to pick up his music career and invented the draft story as a reason to leave the United States. The Selective Service system has no record for Bob, which suggests that he may have never gotton a call-up.

In any case, Bob decided it was time to return to Jamaica. Rita continues: "That was what happened. And he then he got a job at DuPont, DuPont Plaza, one of those big hotels in Delaware, and he was vacuuming one day, he said. And when he got that letter I cried, I really cried. He said he was vacuuming one day and the bag burst with the dust and it flew right up in his face. And he knew that this was the end of it, he was leaving America. He said he wasn't born for that, he think he was born to play music. I said okay, come home now, we will survive, because it was all about going to America for survival. But if that is the survival you're getting, you're better off surviving in Jamaica."

Bob would later portray his time in America as a period of moral education. "I went to the United States. In front of all these buildings, I said to myself 'rasclaat.' They showed me pictures and kept on telling me: 'God is white.' I said to myself: 'What a damned place! The only thing I could be here is a slave.' Those guys believe in money. On their dollars they wrote 'In God We Trust.' I had to choose between this white God and a black Jesus. I have chosen . . ."

Bob would also become skeptical about the institution of marriage. His mother, Cedella, claimed that her son never wanted to be married and felt that he had been tricked into matrimony. She said that he once took his wedding-day photos off the mantelpiece of her home in Delaware and threw them into the trash. Ten years after his first trip to Delaware, Bob said: "Married people are chained. You can't live by strenuous rules other people make. Check out people who are married—weird."

Bob's music was always more romantic than his life. His lyrics celebrated love, and were playful about lust. He wrote of love-making in metaphor—stirring it up, rubbing guava jelly, pouring out sugar. He never forced himself on women in his songs, but often portrayed himself as a figure waiting for the woman to make a move. In his music, he was usually the one crying after women who had left him. But in his life, in his relationships, he could be as cold as a Delaware winter.

An interviewer once asked Bob in the late 1970s: "I understand you're married. Are you married?"

Bob replied, "No."

The interviewer asked, "Do you have any children?"

Bob said, "I have a couple children in Jamaica. I can't deal with the Western ways of life. If I must live by law, it must be the laws of His Majesty [Selassie]. If it's not the laws of His Majesty, then I can make my own law, y'know what I mean? What I know is all of dem laws is making, is men made dem. And I am a man, too. Know what I mean? That mean I don't think it greater than me."

Was Bob a ladies' man or a womanizer? Was he a playa or did he get played? Rita made international headlines in 2004 when she allegedly claimed in an interview with a British tabloid that Bob had once raped her during their marriage. She later suggested her words had been misunderstood. Her book about her time with Bob, *No Woman No Cry*, makes a lesser claim and says she was "almost raped." According to Rita, Bob had come home at some point in the 1970s and she had told him, "I'm not having sex with you." Bob had insisted, "You're my wife and I want you." And so the two had sex. In interviews for this book, Rita made no charges about being raped or almost raped by Bob. He did, how-ever, cheat on her regularly. It's clear that Rita, like the muses who came before her, has a lot of unresolved anger about her tumultuous artist-muse relationship.

KINKY REGGAE

Pop music is often portrayed as godless. Rock has been called the devil's music. Religious groups often fight to keep secular sounds out of their houses of worship. There was resistance to gospel back in the 1940s because it was too bluesy, and in the twenty-first century, there has been resistance to rap in the church because it is too hip-hoppy. Even today, many Jamaican churches won't allow anything in their doors that smacks of reggae.

Is God dead in pop music? No, He's where He's always been—offstage, working in production. The sacred has long shaped popular songwriting. Pop songwriters have been wrestling with issues of sin and salvation since Son House in the 1920s. Blues belter Bessie Smith sang songs of faith. Elvis Presley sang gospel. Aretha Franklin started her career in gospel and returned to the form every few years. Rock bands like U2 have praised God in their songs. R&B mavericks such as Marvin Gaye, Stevie Wonder, and Prince have explored religious themes on their albums. The rap act Public Enemy lyrically embraced the Nation of Islam. And pop icons such as Madonna have turned their careers into spiritual quests. (Perhaps when you have a name like Madonna, you almost have to face up to religious questions at some point.)

No major mainstream artist, however, has created a body of work as deeply religious as Bob Marley's. Many of his songs, and every one of his albums, deal with his faith. And yet few fans view him as a polarizing proselytizer. How Bob could be so religious, and yet come across as so secular, has a lot to do with the nature of the sect he chose to embrace. It also has a lot to do with the brilliant and eccentric producer who helped him reconcile his artistry with his newfound religion: Lee "Scratch" Perry. Few doubt that Bob's faith was genuine. But *The Harder They Come* director Perry Henzell once pointed out that the reggae star's decision to embrace a religious faction that featured ganja as a sacrament may have been the canniest move of his career.

When Bob Marley returned from America to Jamaica in November 1966, two kinds of royalty were on his mind. He desperately wanted to collect the royalties he felt he and his fellow Wailers were owed from Coxson Dodd, the head of Studio One. It rankled Bob that the Wailers had worked so hard at Studio One and recorded so many hits but had made so little money. He wasn't dreaming of riches, but he did want to earn enough to pay for the basic things of life. That was what had driven him to Delaware to find a job outside of the music industry. He thought Coxson was little more than a thief and even told people so. Said Bob: "We gave him four number one tunes in '66 and all we got was twenty pounds each." The need to make money to support his growing family would force him to return to Delaware at least a few more times between 1966 and 1972. Bob had written Bunny in 1966 asking that he and Peter come to the United States so they could all get jobs and relaunch the Wailers in the States.

Bunny didn't like the scheme. He never wrote Bob back. Bob got the message. "I felt that that was a long shot," Bunny argues. Bunny thought the group would be better off courting fans in Jamaica, where they had already established themselves as hit makers. Bob gave up on his plan and came home.

Bob was thinking about another kind of royalty when Rita, Bunny, Peter, and Vision met him at Palisadoes Airport in Kingston. Haile Selassie, emperor of Ethiopia, had visited Jamaica when Bob was in America, and had stepped off a flight at the same airport. The emperor had arrived in Kingston on April 21, 1966. Bunny, Peter, and Rita had all been there to witness the event. Ras Tafari (*Ras* meant "Duke" and *Tafari* was his family name) had assumed the title Emperor Haile Selassie I in November 1930. He claimed to be descended from King Solomon. His coronation ceremony, held in St. George's Cathedral in Addis Ababa, Ethiopia, had been attended by representatives of all the great powers of the day. It was covered by press from around the world. Blacks around the planet took pride in the glory of the event. The emperor was the kind of man who was impressive even in defeat. The captain of a British ship that carried Selassie to a brief exile in England in 1936 before the outbreak of World War II (he returned to power in 1941) said, "I have seldom been so impressed with any man, black or white, and his consideration, courtesy, and above all his dignity, has left a deep impression on every officer and man in my ship."

The emperor is coming! The news spread all over the island in April 1966. The emperor is coming! The visit made Jamaicans feel more important. They walked taller in Ocho Rios. They held their heads a bit higher in Mocho. The imperial visit confirmed the island's place on the map, and its significance in world affairs. Jamaica was important and attention must be paid. The emperor is coming! Men, women, and children came in from the countryside to see His Majesty. Some rode buses, others pedaled bikes; many walked. Some led goats, others came with cows. Some were blind, hoping for miracles. Others were faithless and hoping for revelation. The emperor is coming! Rastas poured into Kingston by the thousands. Spectators took their places along roadsides, on rooftops, on the hoods of cars, in the windows of stores, on the backs of trucks. The emperor is coming!

Selassie was the inspiration for a new religious movement in Jamaica: the Rastifari. Bob once said that he had been a Rasta "since creation." He began thinking seriously about the faith around the late 1960s, before he first traveled to America. His biggest influences, he said, were "the Bible and Haile Selassie. Never have no influence in that same sense." The Wailers' early Trench Town singing mentor, Joe Higgs, had been a Rasta for several years before he began tutoring the group. Rita joined the faith in 1966. She saw the emperor's motorcade as it passed by her on the roadside. She had been a skeptic about his supposed divinity, but then had a vision that day in which she saw stigmata on the emperor's palms. After that, she became a believer. She wrote Bob about her mystical experience and he wrote back to say she was going crazy. Bunny and Peter embraced the faith in the late 1960s. Peter was inspired by Selassie's visit to Jamaica to write and record a song to mark the event: "Rasta Shook Them Up." Declared Bunny: "You had to behold it to reveal it. Because every individual who witnessed it had a total different revelation. Rasta shook them up is the only term that could be used to shorten the description of what really took place. And the Wailers led by Peter said it on record." (The event shook up another important music figure: a young Clive Campbell, who would grow up to become hip-hop pioneer DJ Kool Herc, watched the emperor's arrival on TV in Kingston.)

After Bob's arrival, Bob, Bunny, Rita, and Peter headed from the airport to Trench Town. They took a seat under a tree outside 8 First Street. It was a place the Wailers often went to relax, talk, and play music. They called it Tartar's Ranch or the Casbah. Bob had a new green electric guitar. The other band members took turns admiring it. Spliffs were lit and passed around. They reminisced about the old days. Then Bob unveiled his plan to liberate the Wailers from Coxson and Studio One. Bunny and Peter were overjoyed. They had both had the same idea.

The Rastafari movement has its roots in Bob Marley's home parish of St. Ann. Marcus Mosiah Garvey was born in St. Ann's Bay on August 17, 1887. He was a man of ideals who was always looking for a way to support his high-mindedness with cash; a prophet forever in search of profits. He shifted from job to job. Garvey spent his teen years as a printer's apprentice. He then became a printer. He moved to Kingston at age sixteen and took elocution lessons. He became a journalist for the *Africa Times* and *Orient Review* and traveled the world. He visited South America and Europe and wrote poetry about the things that he saw. When he returned to Jamaica in 1914, he launched the Universal Negro Improvement Association. UNIA's goal was to inspire worldwide black unity, to develop Africa, and to encourage the black arts movement. By the mid-1920s, UNIA had 1,100 branches in more than forty countries. Success brought enemies. Garvey was hounded throughout his life by legal authorities in the United States and Jamaica. His organizations faced and sometimes succumbed to financial pressures. He set up a shipping concern called the Black Star Line to transport people and products between America, the Caribbean, and Africa. The company lasted only three years. It failed, in part, because of determined efforts by the U.S. government to destroy the business. Garvey's policies came under attack from many whites and blacks. W. E. B. DuBois called him a "lunatic or a traitor."

When Emperor Haile Selassie was crowned, Garvey published an article in his Jamaican newspaper, *The Blackman*, that intoned, "Last Sunday, a great ceremony took place at Addis Ababa, the capital of Abyssinia. It was the coronation of the new Emperor of Ethiopia—Ras Tafari . . . We do hope that Ras Tafari will live long to carry out his wonderful intentions . . . The Psalmist prophesied that Princes would come out of Egypt and Ethiopia would stretch out her hands unto God. We have no doubt that the time is now." Garvey died in London in 1940 and his body was returned to Jamaica in 1964, but his words about the coronation began to take on a mythic weight. Legend has it that Garvey said long before the coronation, "Look to the East for the coming of an African King." In 1929, Garvey staged a play in Kingston called *The Coronation of the King and Queen of Africa*. But the source for the famous "look to the East" quote was probably James Morris Webb, a clergyman who published a book in 1919 titled *A Black Man Will Be the Coming Universal King, Proven by Biblical History*. Webb was an associate of Garvey's and spoke at the 1924 UNIA convention. In any case, many Jamaicans began to see the emperor's reign as the fulfillment of Garvey's prophecy.

Jamaica had been abused by the Spanish and colonized by the British; it had been left behind by the industrial revolution, it would shy away from the Communist revolution and it would be spurned by the sexual revolution. The people of the island needed a hero, a savior, a messiah, someone to rescue them from all the things they needed rescuing from. Thousands wanted to be saved—from poverty, from colonialism, from political corruption, from religious hypocrisy, from racial self-hatred. So a savior was found—not by three wise men, but by four. A quartet of Jamaican men—

Leonard Howell, Joseph Hibbert, Archibald Dunkley, and Robert Hinds—all reached the conclusion in the early 1930s that Haile Selassie's coronation had spiritual significance. All four may have been followers of Garvey. All four became ministers in separate groups that claimed that the king of Ethiopia was the messiah.

The new doctrine of Rastafari was incubated in the slums of Kingston in the early 1930s. These areas were populated by thousands of unemployed workers. Many of these men and women had abandoned their farms to find wage labor in the city. They now found themselves landless, jobless, and listless. Wrote the *Daily Gleaner* in 1934: "Hundreds of thousands of our people are mere squatters on properties off which they may be turned at any time . . . There is no hope for the prosperity of the peasants until they are settled on lands of their own . . . There is too much land monopoly in this agricultural society." The new religion had a difficult birth. Its followers were treated like lepers, its leaders were hounded like hucksters. In 1933, Howell was imprisoned for trying to sell five thousand pictures of Haile Selassie that he said were passports to Ethiopia. When he left prison in 1940, he and his followers moved to the remote hills of Jamaica, following in the footsteps of the Maroons.

There is no central, completely agreed-upon Rastafari doctrine. There may be as many views of the sect as there are strains of marijuana. (And perhaps these two points are related.) But the most central tenet of the faith is this: Rastas believe that Haile Selassie is God. Bob philosophized: "I and I is just Rastafari. See Christ when he return [will have] new name. That means Christ when he return on earth 'e wouldn't be Christ—he would 'ave a new name. Now the new name is Rastafari. Now Haile Selassie is Rastafari, and Haile Selassie is earth's rightful ruler . . . if the big people don't see it, the children will." Rastas don't believe in death. Many avoid funerals. "All preachers preach that you must die and go to heaven," Bob asserted. "Now I and I read that the gift of God is ever-livin' life. So we don't see death as a part of life." Rastas see Africa as their true spiritual home and believe that someday they will embark on an exodus and return. Rastafari represented a spiritual challenge to the colonial mind-set. Klaus de Albuquerque once labeled Jamaica a "pigmentocracy" in which "blackness became equated with lowliness and servility, whiteness with power and godliness." Rastafari preached that the Messiah was black and the heart of darkness, Africa, was paradise. It was a strong, simple message that cut through the island's complexion complex. As Bob put it: "What happen is we in Jamaica, is our history is we come from Africa. After a period of time, over four hundred years, we get to move on our own destiny, which is African. We don't feel ourselves governed by Queen Elizabeth's law." Rastafari became the religion of the oppressed, the dispossessed, and the falsely accused. Rastas used the term "Babylon" to refer to Western culture in general. Young people in Jamaica were especially attracted to the new religion. Bob predicted that "every youth them kill upon the street, whether him have dreadlocks, as long as 'im a youth, is a Rasta dem kill because if him grow and mature, 'im gonna be a Rasta. But them try and kill them young. They say kill them before they grow." One of the early slogans of the Rastas was "Your mother forsake you, your father forsake you, Rasta will take you."

The Rastas were, at first, regarded as mere curiosities, something to see on the way to Montego Bay or on the road back from Dunn's River Falls. They were the Jamaican version of bearded ladies or the Hottentot Venus. They were religious misfits who wore their freak flags on their heads for all to see. Travel writer Patrick Leigh Fermor wrote in his book *The Traveller's Tree: Island Hopping Through the Caribbean in the 1940s* that "Jamaica is bewilderingly prolific in unusual groups of human beings . . . none of them more peculiar than the Rastafari—a thoroughly eccentric movement named after the Emperor of Abyssinia . . . The Rastafari live in a patch of waste land by the railway in the western slums of Kingston known as the Dunghill. From flagpoles above their hovels flutter the red, yellow and green tricolour flags of Abyssinia, and notice boards bear messages in clumsily-formed letters, which say 'Long Live Abyssinia' or 'We are Ethiopians.' "

Fermor went on: "It was plain to see that the Negroes lounging among the trees and huts regarded [my] white intrusion with extreme dislike. They [had] expressions of really frightening depravity. All were dressed in the most sordid rags, and all equipped with curling black beards." Later, Fermor entered a Rasta hut: "The hut was about two yards square and constructed entirely of copies of the *Daily Gleaner* glued together . . . A photograph of [Selassie], nursing a battered lap-dog with enormous eyes, was stuck to the paper wall. Underneath it in charcoal was written: 'My one hope.' "

The most obvious identifying characteristic of Rastas is their hair. By the 1990s, dreadlocks were everywhere—tucked beneath the caps of baseball players, draped over the furrowed brows of Nobel Prize laureates, tied up behind the ears of political commentators on Fox News. But at first, the hair choices of the Rasta brethren were seen as frightening to children, destabilizing to society, and possibly even sacrilegious. In the 1930s, most male Jamaicans were clean-shaven. Beards were seen as unprofessional and unkempt. The early Rastas grew long curling beards and were nicknamed "beards" or "locksmen." In the 1940s, a small group of young Rastas led by a man named Wato began growing dreadlocks. The move was biblically inspired. Leviticus 21:5 reads: "They shall not make baldness upon their head, neither shall they shave off the corner of their beard nor make any cutting in their flesh." And Judges 16:16 says: "If I be shaven, then my strength will go from me and I shall become weak and be like any other man." Bob spelled out the teachings: "Our lawgiver is Moses . . . When you take a vow to be a [Rasta], which is African, then you shall let no comb nor razor come up on your hair and you shall let the locks of your hair grow. Now this is the locks of my hair, so this just going by the Bible. Everything we do is not a self-taught thing, you know. It's both your conscience and the Bible."

Rastas did not invent dreadlocks. The term *dread* was at first hurled at Rastas as an insult, but was then embraced by the Rastas themselves. Some experts argue that ancient Egyptians may have worn the hairstyle. Whether this is wishful thinking on the part of Afrocentrists, or a laudably forward-thinking fashion choice on the part of some pharaohs, is unclear. Ancient Roman accounts describe the Celts as having "hair like snakes." Bahatowie priests of the Ethiopian Coptic Church wore locked hair in the fifth century. East Indians brought to Jamaica in the nineteenth century to cultivate sugar, coffee, and cocoa may have brought the practice of locked hair to the island. A photograph confirms that sadhus, Indian holy men who wore locked hair, were present on the island in 1910. Around the time the Rasta movement was spreading in the 1940s and 1950s, the Mau Mau rebellion against the British in Kenya was receiving coverage in newspapers around the world. The warriors who led the uprising, the Kikuyu freedom fighters, wore their hair in locks to frighten their enemies. They may also have inspired the hairstyles of the early Rastas.

No care is required to cultivate dreadlocks. Any hair, regardless of texture, will eventually "lock" if the hair is not combed or brushed. Bob complained: "Plenty people have the wrong idea about this locks thing. Like I read in a magazine: 'Marley came onstage with his waxed locks.' Now that is very much a lie, because I could never sit down and put wax on my 'air, my wool, to keep it together. It would be clammy and stink, mon. Them blind, mon! This come natural." The new style both frightened and fascinated outsiders. The book *Ian Fleming Introduces Jamaica*—penned in part by the man who created James Bond—featured photographs glorifying Rastas and their locks. One popular Jamaican anecdote offers another perspective. A lady was walking through downtown Kingston, the tale goes, when she turned a corner and ran into a Dread going in the opposite direction. "Jesus!" the woman exclaimed. The Dread put a finger to his mouth and replied, "Shhh! Tell no one thou hast seen I!"

Politicians, the public, and the press didn't know exactly what to make of the Rastafari. In the 1940s, Rastas were sometimes rounded up and forcibly shaved. On July 12, 1941, the *Jamaica Times* reported that people caught on Rasta lands in the mountains were being flogged and that the attacks "bore a close resemblance to the ruthless Maroon era." One of the first articles to mention Rastas in the *Daily Gleaner* was about a satirical play that mocked the movement. The *Daily Gleaner* of Monday, February 13, 1950, announced: "Bim and Bam, popular comedians and show promoters, will present another dynamic show—*Finger in the Ink*—which opens at the Ward Theatre on Wednesday. This show, which is based on the recent general elections is jampacked with laughs, songs, music and dances . . . Bim will appear as a census taker, P.N.P. candidate, and the Minister of Comedy. Bam plays the parts of a Rastafari Man, J.L.P. Candidate, and the Member of Central Kingston."

Rastas—who didn't recognize the legitimacy of the government—represented a threat to the legal establishment in Jamaica. Judges routinely remanded Rastas for medical examination. The *Daily Gleaner* of Friday, June 9, 1950, reported: "Court Admonishes 'Rastafari' Men . . . The men caused further disturbances in court as they showed reluctance in kissing the Bible preferring to swear in the language of their cult . . . All four gave evidence that they had caused no upset . . . as they had only gone to the House with a flag to demonstrate that they wanted to go 'back home to Africa.' The Magistrate informed them that they could not go back to a place from which they had never come."

As the ranks of Rastas grew, the notices in the local papers grew more alarmist. The *Star* of March 24, 1958, reported: "The city of Kingston was 'captured' near dawn on Saturday by some 300 bearded men of the Rastafarian cult along with their women and children. About 3 A.M. early marketgoers saw members of the Rastafarian movement gathered in the center of Victoria Park, with towering poles, atop of which, fluttered black, green and red banners, and loudly proclaiming that they had captured the city . . . When the police moved towards them, a leader of the group with his hands raised issued a warning to the police: 'touch not the Lord's anointed.' . . . The police finally moved them."

When Marley embraced the Rasta way, he was taking on trouble. Rasta musicians were routinely targeted by cops. Bunny, Peter, and Bob would all spend time in Jamaican prisons for marijuana offenses. Toots Hibbert of the Maytals spent two years in jail for marijuana possession, nearly derailing his career. He later wrote the hit song "54–46 (That's My Number)" about the experience. Bob started up dreads, let them revert into an Afro, and then let his dreads grow again. During a 1968 Independence Day concert at the Regal Theatre in Kingston, he strode out in Rastaman garb and sandals and was booed and mocked by some in the audience. The other acts were in fitted costumes and suits. Bob Marley going Rasta in Jamaica was akin to Bob Dylan plugging in his instruments at the Newport Folk Festival in 1965. It was more than a simple change of style; it represented a cultural shift.

Among many Jamaicans—and some Americans—the Rasta movement struck a chord. Alice Walker, author of *The Color Purple*, was seduced by the sexual allure of dreadlocks. "What would it be like to make love to someone with hair on your head like that, and to be made love to by someone with hair on his or her head like that?" Walker wondered in an essay. "It must be like the mating of two lions, I thought. Aroused." Walker eventually began wearing dreadlocks herself. Wrote Walker, "Bob Marley is the person who taught me to trust the universe enough to respect my hair." Black journalist Wanda Coleman interviewed Bob Marley for a small publication in the early seventies, and fell in love with the group's music and style. "Not just Marley but big-faced Bunny as well," Coleman enthused. "And I fell in love with Peter Tosh on sight. Jah was he gorgeous, I wanted to let my hair dread immediately. I didn't go dread right away because I had to maintain an appearance at least marginally acceptable to mainstream society. As it has turned out, when my hair dreads, as it eventually did on its own following the death of my father, it locks up into an odd variety of clumps that look, for all the world, like buds of dried dark brown marijuana."

But most Jamaicans in the 1970s viewed Rastas as outcasts. They were seen as "dutty," or dirty. Cedella Marley, Bob's eldest daughter, said she had trying times as a Rasta kid in Jamaica in the early 1970s. Her father's status as a musician did not shield his children from taunts. In fact, his local fame made it worse. People who didn't know Bob mocked her for looking weird, people who knew Bob attacked her for her family's seeming success. Her locks made her an easy target, marking her as a Rastafari and linking her to her father. "In Jamaica, being Rastafarian, you were looked down upon, it wasn't like you were welcome anywhere," Cedella explains. "We were shunned by a lot of people. I remember having friends and wanting to invite them over to the house and they'd have to lie to their parents that they were going to spend a weekend at this other friend's house because the parent would never have them stay at my house."

Coxson Dodd was not a Rasta. He didn't particularly care for Rasta themes in music. His rival, Duke Reid, outright banned Rasta theology in records put out by his label, Treasure Isle. He even promoted songs that were harshly critical of rude boys and Rasta such as Bob Andy's 1966 anti-Rudie song "Crime Don't Pay." It was a decision that would, in part, lead to a decline in Reid's fortunes. Rasta was the future. Coxson, for his part, tolerated instrumental records with Rasta themes. Coxson gave the green light to Don Drummond's "The Reburial" (a wordless tribute to Marcus Garvey's body returning home to Jamaica), and he also released Delroy Wilson's Rasta-themed "Lion of Judah," which was written by an up-and-comer named Lee "Scratch" Perry. But Studio One was slow to catch on to the emerging new force. Said Scratch: "Nah, Coxson don't have anything to do with them type of things. Coxson don't like Rasta."

But the Rasta influence could not be ignored or denied. Rasta meetings—called grounations—featured drumming and chanting. The drums employed were of varying sizes—the bass, the funde, and the repeater. The sound of Rasta chants and drumming was finding its way onto the Jamaican pop charts in the 1960s. As early as 1960, the Folkes Brothers had scored a hit with "Oh Carolina," which had been inspired by Rasta percussion. The Wailers were on the cutting edge of the Rasta musical movement. The group's 1966 song "Who Feels It Knows It," recorded while Bob was in America, used the Rasta phrase "I and I" for the first time in a recorded song. "I and I" is the Rasta way of indicating that God and the self are linked.

The Wailers and Coxson were heading in different directions. The band wanted more money and more creative freedom. Coxson was looking to exert even more control over the artists on his label. Still, he wanted to work with Bob, whom he regarded as a tremendous talent. When the reconstituted Wailers went to meet with him, Coxson had an offer. Studio One's records were distributed in England by Island Records, which was headed up by a young white Jamaican entrepreneur named Chris Blackwell. Said Bunny: "Coxson, desperately trying to entice Bob to work for him again, played his final stunt by inventing a trick to say that Blackwell had sent some royalties from England for the Wailers. This amount was less than a hundred pounds. And weekly salaries were deducted from it, leaving almost nothing. We were expecting the same old Jackson as tight as ever."

The Wailers took what little money was left. They needed it. Then they told Coxson about their new demand. They were launching their own label and they wanted to rent Studio One to record their music. Bob put the decision in context: "That's a big move, in Jamaica. Prince Buster was the first to start the revolution by leaving the producers and doing it himself. Then myself, then Lee Perry . . . and you can't count the rest." The Wailers knew little about how the record business actually worked. But they decided the way to make money was to control the whole process. Bob reasoned: "It's better to know for yourself if your record is a flop than have someone else tell you. And if your record sells good, the producer pretends he's gone to Nassau when you come by the office. In Jamaica, you're expected to use your knife, or your machete, or your gun."

The Wailers named their new venture Wail 'N' Soul 'M Records. The logo for the new label was three interlocked hands symbolizing Bob, Bunny, and Peter. They set up a small shop in Trench Town to sell the records, which were delivered via bicycle. Cedella Marley said: "We lived in Trench Town too for a while. We lived right in front of a cemetery, which was weird. And I remember going to other people's funerals who I didn't know, just to go. Dad was always at the record shop, him and Mom. It was like a business with them—we got to go to this studio and try to get this record done. There was no violence. It was pretty calm in Trench Town during those days."

The Wailers rented time at Studio One to record a song that Bob had written in America. It was called "Bend Down Low." The song was a huge hit—but the Wailers saw very little of the money. The Wailers suspected that other record producers were selling bootlegged copies of their hit. "I thought me no gonna work for no one again," Bob said, "so we split from Coxson we form Wailin' Soul, but like, I don't know about the business, and me get caught again. 'Bend Down Low' was number one in Jamaica at the time, but them press it and sell it—it was a black-market type of business."

The Wailers needed to find a new way to get their music to the people.

Like Bob, Bunny, and Peter, Lee "Scratch" Perry was from the countryside. He was born Hugh Rainford Perry on March 26, 1936, in Hanover, Jamaica. He got the pet name of Lee from his mother. He hated school. He never reached past the equivalent of fourth grade. "From school days, I was learning more from comics than from school," Scratch recounts. "I always borrowed the comic books about good over evil. And I always read about the heroes and I worship the heroes. My number one comic was *Superman, Batman and Robin, Iron Man*." Iron Man made his first appearance in 1963, so Scratch had an extended childhood.

Scratch likes to laugh. He likes to giggle. He enjoys provocation. He has an impish tone in his voice. He will say odd things that he may or may not believe. He says, for example, that he is descended from King David. That might be possible to believe. But Scratch says the familial connection is quite close, and that King David is his great-grandfather. That is considerably harder to believe. Scratch enjoys the appearance of insanity. It is why his recordings break so sharply with the mainstream. Scratch swims in a different stream. "I have personal contact with God," Scratch proclaims. "And the God that I know is rain. Rainwater. River water. Seawater. And pipe water. That's my God. And I am a fish. I am a fish being. Not really a human being. It may sound funny to you, but I'm not really a human being, I'm a fish being."

Scratch decided as a young man that he would earn money from having fun. He became a dominoes champ. He also became a dance champion. He would travel to various dance competitions held during sugarcane-harvesting season. He would move his body to boogie-woogie and blues and jazz. He was especially skilled at a herky-jerky style of dance named "the Yank." He decided to move to Kingston and get involved in the record industry. "I wanted to make the kind of music I wanted to dance to," he explains. The first image he can remember from his arrival in Kingston is a picture of Marcus Garvey.

Scratch first started working for Duke Reid, then decided he preferred to work for the underdog, Coxson. He was frustrated, however, by his limited role at Studio One. He wanted more of an outlet for his creative abilities. Coxson didn't like his voice and gave songs that Scratch wrote to other performers. Bemoans Scratch: "He was kind of seeing me as his handyman. He wasn't even paying me no sensible money, just a small money, because me come from the country and me is country bwoy, so me don't know money or something like that. Me give him words and tell him words to fight against Prince Buster and Duke Reid and he get Delroy Wilson sing it. So I was a very good help to him and he never want me to be an artist or a singer or anything like that." But he kept hounding Coxson and fought his way into becoming a producer. His 1961 song "Chicken Scratch" gave him his nickname. Scratch soon rebelled against Coxson's leadership. He recorded "Give Me Justice," a song bashing Coxson. He recorded it at Studio One when his boss was out. It was the first of many tracks that Scratch would record in which he lashed out at former employers. "Well, working for Coxson was like slavery," Scratch laments. "I wanted to get in the business, and have to make a sacrifice to get in the business." He later went to work for another producer, Joe Gibbs, the head of the Amalgamated record label. He came out with the song "I Am the Upsetter"—another anti-Coxson single. Not long afterward, he broke with Gibbs and released "People Funny Boy"—a song that savaged Gibbs. It was a huge hit, selling more than sixty thousand copies in its initial release. Scratch sums it up: "Me go to the studio, and say, Well, me want to speak my mind, so I speak my mind."

Scratch found the Wailers intriguing. Fascinating even. And a real challenge. He saw them as true rebels. He just thought they needed guidance. But Scratch, at the time, was having great success in Jamaica and England with a series of instrumentals. He wasn't looking to work with singers. Scratch recollects: "I did not want to work with them, they want to work with me. Bob come to me and ask me, I did not go to them and ask them. We were making a series of instrumentals and the Wailers weren't making anything, they was singing for Coxson Downbeat. And after them finished, them didn't go any further. Bob understand that I am on top, so he come here and ask me he want to work with me."

Scratch's independence—and his production skills—impressed the Wailers. "Scratch was the only artist, other than the Wailers, who had left Coxson and was capable of running an independent record business," Bunny contends. Scratch immediately focused in on his new prize pupils. One of the first things he recognized was that he was dealing with three stars. They had three dynamic talents that were capable of working independently. Together, however, they were magic. Scratch was sure to give each Wailer a starring role. He had Peter take the lead vocals on "Brand New Second Hand" and "400 Years." He had Bunny step to the front on the lyrical ballad "Dreamland." And he had Bob take the central role on such songs as "Soul Rebel" and "Satisfy My Soul." The other two Wailers would sing backup while one group member handled the lead. Everyone was kept happy and laughing and satisfied.

Jamaican music was changing. Coxson and Reid and the old guard were resisting it, but Scratch was eager for the future. In fact, the Upsetter was one of the forces dragging the music in a new direction. Bob was also pushing for a shift. "You find we in Jamaica, the guys that own the record company capitalize on the music too much," Bob once remarked. "So as the years go by we have to change the music so we can stay in business. Because we don't want no record company, all we want is the music." An unusually warm summer in 1966 had made it too hot to dance to ska. The slower, sweeter rhythms of rock steady were the rage from 1966 until the end of 1968. Scratch's "People Funny Boy" helped usher in a new beat. The song used the sound of a crying baby in its refrain, a creative touch that set it apart from pop trifles on the radio. (It also prefigured the use of samples in hip-hop.) The tune employed guitars that were used rhythmically and not strictly melodically. The bass line was heavier and more driving than was typical in Jamaican music up to that point. "It was funny. It was something different. It wasn't a ska, and it wasn't a rock steady," Scratch comments. Another song, "Do the Reggay," released by Toots and the Maytals in August 1968, helped give the new genre a name: reggae. Contends Scratch: "['People Funny Boy'] was spiritual vibration of what come to be called reggae now, that what create it."

Jamaica had found a new rhythm. On September 7, 1968, the

Rainbow Club in Kingston took out an ad in the *Daily Gleaner* announcing "Come do this Brand new Dance: The Reggae." Ranglin, who had performed on the first ska recordings, also played guitar on some of the very first reggae songs. "I think it's a thing that's connected to climate," Ranglin supposes. He says he arranged the ska music for Millie Small's "My Boy Lollipop" at a fast tempo because he recorded it in England during the winter and "people need something to keep the circulation going." But he didn't think that kind of quick pace would work for Jamaica—the country was too hot. Rock steady was a more suitable music—perfect for enjoying under a shade tree when the day was hot. But what should people listen to on moderately warm days? "So this is why I came up with a beat now in the middle of that that's a little slower than the ska, a little faster than the rock steady," Ranglin says, laughing.

The origin of the word *reggae* is unclear. Why did Toots first exhort listeners to "Do the Reggay"? Toots said the word comes from what men would call good-looking women. Remarks Toots: "Girl was looking good—say streggay. It was just a word. After a while it become great." Ranglin said the name was a reaction to the rhythm. "I wasn't the one that gave it a name," he admits. "But some people came in the studio and I heard them saying 'a-reggay, a-reggay' and that's how the beat came in. So I say I want to give a lot of praise to the drummer, Hugh Malcolm, because he was the one who had that lovely beat." Whatever the origins of the name, Bob saw the music as "a heavy-duty machine" that could carry weighty spiritual messages, proclaiming, "What happens to them is, the more reggae you play, the more Rasta you have. So if we play more disco, then we'll have more eyebrow pencil and lipstick. You hear me? The more reggae you play, the more Rasta you have, the more disco you play, the more fantasy you get." Scratch also saw the cultural potential of the new music. He said he wasn't a reggae man at the start of his career. He was a soul man. But when he looked around him in Jamaica, all he saw was people suffering. And he came to believe that only reggae could help the sufferers.

A new sound required a new band. For inspiration, Scratch reached back into his days as a youth reading comic books. He started thinking about the basic conflict in most comic books: good versus evil. He wanted to capture that. He wanted a band that would represent that. So he named his group the Upsetters. He was the chief Upsetter, so they would be his team. Together they would tip the balance for good. The Upsetters were a loosely organized group, with a shifting membership. The core of the group was drawn from the band the Hippy Boys, which featured Glenroy Adams on keyboards, Alva "Reggie" Lewis on guitar, Carlton "Carly" Barrett on drums, and Aston "Family Man" Barrett on bass.

Family Man got his start in music as a child by making a bass guitar out of a two-by-four. He would play it in the back room of his mother's house. Carly fashioned a drum set out of old paint cans and would accompany his brother. Family Man was said to have gotten his nickname because he had fathered many children. He tells a different story: "Family Man—I label myself in my early years in the music. Because I am the one who get that extra inspiration from the Almighty. So I always getting some youth together and we get pieces of things to make instrument. We make music out of nothing. And I say I want to think of a different kind of term. I don't want to say I am the leader or the foreman or the boss or the one in charge of everybody. We all have to live together and play the music as a family. But the one who is in charge of that gets to be the Family Man. And the name become a legend." The rhythm section was a key component of the new reggae sound. Bob personally recruited Family Man to be part of his recording sessions with Scratch. He had heard Family Man's bass lines on the radio. They were strange—whimsical and melodious; the lines anchored songs and took them to new places, too. It was what Bob was looking for. He asked Reggie to track down Family Man for a recording session. Reggie got in touch with him and told him to meet Bob at night in an alley behind Harring Street in downtown Kingston. Family Man, eager for a paying gig, agreed. He and Bob came face-to-face. Reggie left Bob and Family Man to converse.

"Talk to him, I soon come back," Reggie said.

But Bob didn't sit down and talk to Family Man. Instead, he attended to other business. Family Man lit a spliff while he was waiting. Twenty minutes later, Reggie came back.

"What happened, man?" Bob said to Reggie. "I asked you to do me a favor."

"What?" said Reggie.

"I asked you to get this musician man for me."

"I bring the man come long time."

"Where the man is?"

"That the man sitting over there!"

Bob walked over to Family Man, who was a teenager at the time.

"You mean this youth here? And him name Family Man who play all of these bass lines what I been hearing?"

Family Man decided it was time to speak up. "Yes," he said.

The bass lines Bob had been hearing on the radio sounded like the work of a veteran musician. He thought Family Man—in part because of the nickname—was a much older man. But Family Man was only one year younger than Bob.

Bob smiled. He said: "If it really you play that, you're the right man den."

Said Family Man later: "And we been together straight until the passing of Bob."

Scratch said when Bob Marley first came to him he wanted to sound like James Brown. On "Black Progress," a song Bob performed with the Upsetter band, he actually shouts, à la James Brown, "I'm black and I'm proud!" Drawing on his contact with black autoworkers in America, he began dressing hipper, with berets and flared pants. His style became somewhat theatrical. It looked like he was auditioning for a musical about the Black Panthers. Scratch didn't think this was the right direction for him. Why echo Americans? Why not try something new? He wanted Bob's music to focus less on soul and more on spirit. "We take it to a spiritual level," Scratch discloses. "Because him did not have any songs that could hit international or any songs of spiritual size. So me take him into a zone and start to take him into the Bible, and into a spiritual level and start to create those vibration for him, and that what the people them want to hear." Scratch prodded Bob to question his world more. Said Bob: "You gotta check the psychology behind everything. Why is this? Why is that? You have to ask questions."

Scratch was a Rasta, but he didn't look like one. He didn't wear dreadlocks. Giggling, Scratch says, "Not in the hair. Not in the locks. I don't believe too much in the locks. Good for catching girls. I don't think I'm from that tribe." Scratch had been present when Haile Selassie visited Kingston. "I was living on the street where the emperor have to pass coming from the airport," he recounts. "So I didn't have to go to the airport. I was up standing by at the roadside where I live. I was living at Water Street. And the emperor pass by my street to go to Kingston to go into the town."

The emperor is here! Scratch stood on his toes, trying to peek above the heads of the other crowd members. His eyes opened wide when he saw the emperor. He was not a giant. He was a small man, just like Scratch. He looked like a figurine. He was only a little bit bigger than the souvenirs being sold along the roadway! Scratch was far from disappointed by this development—he was elated. The diminutive producer came from a long line of admittedly "wee people." The fact that the emperor—an indisputably important man—was the size of "a dolly" meant that there was hope for everyone. Greatness wasn't about size. This truly was a king. This was the man everyone had been waiting for all these years. Happiness washed over Scratch like a warm wave over the sand. After the visit, Scratch painted the emperor's name on the front of his house. After he did it, he said, lightning flashed in the sky.

The first song Scratch recorded with Bob was a track called "My Cup." Said Bob: "It wasn't very big, but it appealed to a certain taste." Then Scratch reached into his bag of tricks. He had often found success in attacking his old employers. He encouraged Bob to record a song called "Small Axe." The central idea of the song was that a small ax can fell a big tree. But the lyric was also a pun. It was an attack on the three biggest record producers at the time—the big t'ree. " 'Small Axe' was about righteousness against sin," Bob explained. "It didn't encourage violence. It didn't mean you should go out and cut a man down, it was a power, a world power. It's a victory. It's a Small Axe." Said Bunny: "A lot of fans might have thought we were referring to the tree that you would plant and grow, but the three was directed at the Duke [Reid], the Prince [Buster], and the Sir [Coxson]."

Another landmark Scratch production was "Duppy Conquerer." Family Man was not on the first recorded version of the song. Scratch said he only had enough money for studio time and not for musicians. Family Man refused to play without pay up front. The tune was recorded without him. Afterward, Scratch played Family Man what he had recorded. "I tell him that it's a good rhythm, but that rhythm there is not for 'Duppy Conquerer,' " Family Man recalls. "You have to go back to the studio." The new version was cut in two hours, but the engineer refused to hand over the master, claiming that the studio time hadn't been paid for. This time, apparently, Scratch had paid for the musicians and not the studio time. Bunny grabbed a piece of wood and threatened the engineer's life. The tape was released. "Duppy Conquerer" went on to become a number one record in Jamaica. Its appeal rested, in part, on its evocation of Jamaican myth. Duppy tales—ghost stories—are popular throughout Jamaica. The song was about being liberated from prisons—real ones and spiritual ones. Said Bob: "Yeah, it was in those realms. It was really for every prisoner who came out at that time, because it was so good just to be back on the street again."

The Wailers recorded dozens of songs with Scratch between 1970 and 1971. They collaborated on two albums, *Soul Rebel* and *Soul Revolution*. The Wailers started a new label called Tuff Gong. Friends called Bob "Tuff Gong." (One of the early Rasta leaders, Leonard Howell, had been nicknamed "Gong.") Scratch produced the label's first release, "Trench Town Rock." It was another number one hit. The Wailers were at the height of their creative powers during this period. Scratch's productions combined earthy beats with extraterrestrial flourishes. His work was brilliantly thought out and executed, but entirely unfussy-sounding. The music was as lean and hungry as a roadside goat. And Bob had found his lyrical groove. His words were rooted in ordinary experiences—smoking herb, being released from jail, dealing with untrustworthy friends. But his songs were shot through with shock waves of social upheaval and pangs of spiritual yearning. Scratch had seen the emperor's arrival; Bob had not. But who feels it, knows it. The music the Wailers and Scratch made together captured the thrill of revelation. It was as if, when Bob sang, the emperor were always arriving. The Wailers' music, however, is bigger than any sect. Bob's raw emotion draws you in, regardless of denomination.

This was music for Rastas and rudies, saints and sinners, people who marched to a different drummer and folks who just wanted to dance. On one cut, "All in One," Scratch took several of the Wailers' past hits—"Bend Down Low," "Nice Time," "One Love," "Simmer Down," "It Hurts to Be Alone," "Lonesome Feeling"—and connected them into one seamless song. It's a joyous medley that shifts moods with ease, all with a mesmerizing groove. It was proof of the Wailers' mastery and Scratch's wizardry.

But once again, the Wailers were dissatisfied with the amount of money they were getting for their work. "I am not a businessman," Scratch says with a shrug. "But that is why we break up. Because the music was getting somewhere, and dem weren't getting any of the money, something like that I think. As much as they think they should get."

Bunny said Scratch began to change. The Wailers felt they had helped his career. But he seemed to be getting full of himself. Notes Bunny: "Now he profiled like a boss." Bunny also said that the Wailers had agreed to a fifty-fifty split of profits with Scratch. Bunny felt that the agreement wasn't honored. "Scratch now forfeited the agreement by offering us a ten percent royalty instead," Bunny contends. "This was my breaking point."

Bob, Bunny, and Peter met Scratch at the Sombrero Club in Kingston. It was a party to celebrate the band's good fortunes. Everyone seemed to be in a festive mood. Bob and Scratch were deep in conversation as usual. Then Bunny noticed Bob's countenance change. He put on a "screwface," or angry look. Bunny drew closer to find out what the argument was about. Comments

Bunny: "When I heard Bob telling Scratch that our arrangement was fifty-fifty, then I realized what they must have been talking about. Because it also concerned the Wailers, I tried to inquire as to what the argument was about. Then Scratch said in exact words, 'Bunny, me never talk to you, y'know.' " Bunny was not going to let a wee little producer, no matter how talented, turn his back on him. He threw a punch, "leaving the chicken sprawled out all over the floor of the Sombrero Club."

After tempers had cooled somewhat, Scratch and the Wailers decided to have a business summit. The meeting took place at Scratch's Upsetter Record Store on Charles Street. Bob, Bunny, Peter, and Scratch all sat down around a small table in Scratch's office. Scratch asked his wife, Pauline, to bring him a small bottle from his car. The Wailers took note of the strange delivery. There was some sort of yellow lotion or liquid in the bottle. Peter, suspicious, picked it up. Scratch seemed to be nervous about Peter handling it and asked him to leave it alone.

This struck Bunny as odd. Why would Scratch send for a bottle and then get nervous about someone else handling it? What was his game? What was in that bottle? Peter wondered what was going on as well. Was there a genie in the bottle? He started to take off the top, but Scratch quickly stopped him. There was acid in the bottle, Scratch announced. Peter did not believe him and wanted to test it. Scratch told him to put the bottle away. Peter eventually did. Bunny was disgusted that Scratch would resort to such a mean weapon. Fists were one thing; machetes were another. But acid? "We now wanted to be done with Scratch for all times," Bunny reported. "Because if that was what he had in store for the Wailers, then there could have been an ugly scratch from the chicken that the Wailers had feathered and fattened." The Wailers/Upsetter combination was broken.

Scratch said Bunny was the main reason for the breakup. He

also acknowledges that his mystery bottle did contain acid. Said Scratch: "Well, it wasn't made up. Bunny Wailer just getting jealous. And he was trying to encourage Peter Tosh. Him can't fight, Bunny Wailer. But me, me's a cruel man. Me threaten them with acid. It's true. Nah. I am not joker. Anything me say I'm gonna do, me gonna do. Me the Upsetter. Me really have acid. Me is country man. Me don't want to hire gunman, have to pay gunman, and if you don't pay gunman, another gunman gonna kill you. So me believe in self-defense."

Later in his career, Scratch's eccentricities would get the best of him. In the late seventies, he covered his studio, Black Ark, with bizarre graffiti. Then he carefully crossed out the same letters in each of the words he had written on the walls. To scare off other Rastas, he put a pound of pork on the antennae of his car and kept it there until it was infested with maggots and rotted off. He was seen walking backward around Kingston. He asked one visitor to bring him a bunch of green bananas every day so he could pray to them.

In 1981, Henry W. Targowski wrote a detailed account of meeting Scratch in an article published in the Dutch magazine *Vinyl*. Targowski had paid a visit to Scratch hoping to secure a deal to distribute some of his songs on a new label called Black Star Liner, named after Garvey's famous shipping venture. Targowski wrote: "Scratch invited me to follow him into the inner sanctum of the Black Ark. The colorful paintings which had decorated the outer wall of his studio were all gone; Scratch had covered them over with splotches of ugly green and sh—brown paint. Black graffiti had been scribbled in felt-tip over everything. When I entered the studio, the inside décor proved to be an even greater shock: The place was a disaster area. Bits of equipment lay scattered around the room; shelves had been torn down. Boxes of recording tape lay strewn in a jumbled heap in the middle of the floor . . . The inside walls had become a wild montage: the previous art had been painted over with the same green and brown as outside; Scratch had also glued records, metal stampers, tapes and other assorted objects to the walls—layers upon layers of paint and posters and book pages, a chronological history of Scratch's mental state . . . the horrible smell coming from an overflowing septic tank added to the feeling of discomfort . . . Scratch proceeded to give me his rap: he was the 'Lord Thunder Black' and his black footprints of Time trod upon the rainbow. Scratch went on about his mission on earth, how he had been entrusted with the job of protecting the 'original Jah Soundtrack', guarding it from violation by the profane." In 1983, Scratch's studio, Black Ark, burned to the ground. He was held on an arson charge and let go. He later admitted to journalists that he had started the fire himself. He explained that he had realized he must be white, otherwise why would people—such as his ex-wife, Pauline, and Bob Marley—treat him so poorly?

The Wailers had failed to find lasting success with the best producer in Jamaica.

They would turn to America, and Sweden, for help.

MIDNIGHT RAVERS

B ob Marley and his guitar were always in demand at Rasta celebrations. When Mortimer Planno, a Rasta elder, held meetings, Bob was often in attendance, providing a soundtrack to the religious gatherings. Planno had made his name on the day Haile Selassie came to Jamaica. Rastas had surrounded the imperial plane, chanting, singing, and smoking spliffs. It was unclear what the emperor made of the scene. Planno escorted Haile Selassie from his aircraft. For years afterward, Planno made a habit of giving guests huge blowups of a photo of him beside the emperor. To some Rastas, it was a bit like one of the twelve apostles handing out copies of da Vinci's *The Last Supper*. (Exactly which apostle depended on your take on Planno.)

One night in early 1967, the American singer Johnny Nash was at Planno's place to observe a grounation. Nash was a pop-soul singer who was being marketed as the next Johnny Mathis. Trouble was, many young black record buyers weren't all that high on the first Johnny Mathis. So Nash, though he had a solid audience in pop, had trouble connecting with black audiences. He traveled quite a bit, searching for new fans and looking for himself as well. Nash hailed from Houston, Texas, but had adopted Jamaica as a second home. He enjoyed the weather, loved the music, and was fascinated by the people. Bob had heard of Nash—he had scored hits in the U.S. and the U.K. and had appeared in TV shows and movies—but he wasn't all that impressed. "We knew of Johnny Nash in Jamaica before he arrived, but we didn't love him that much," Bob was once quoted as saying. "We appreciated him singing the kind of music he does—he was the first U.S. artist to do reggae—but he isn't really our idol. That's Otis [Redding] or James Brown or [Wilson] Pickett, the people who work it more hard." Bob may not have been a fan of Nash, but Nash quickly became an admirer of Bob's. Bob played a few songs for him at the gathering. Nash came away raving about Bob's talent. He immediately went home and told his friend and business partner, Danny Sims.

Sims was another African-American who had fallen in love with Jamaica. It's a common affliction among foreign visitors—from Ian Fleming (the creator of James Bond, who had several houses on the island) to Sinéad O'Connor (who recorded a reggae album in Bob's old studio), outsiders have come to Jamaica and staked a claim to part of the culture for themselves. Jamaica, to outsiders, seems exotic, but not alien. Jamaicans are rarely rude to foreigners even when they despise them. Who else is going to fill up all the taxis, hotels, and restaurants? Jamaicans have their own language, but it resembles English closely enough—especially when spoken slowly—to make folks from the English-speaking world feel at home. Speech patterns on the island tilt toward friendliness. Rastas reject words like *you*, *me*, *we*, and *they* as divisive and replace them with *I and I*. The phrase signifies togetherness—between people, and between humankind and

God. There's a related term in the local lingo: *irie*. It's a versatile aloha-like word that can mean hello or good-bye. It can be an adjective meaning "great" or a statement: "How are you doing?" "Irie, mon!" Jamaicans have a lot of good reasons to be angry, but they often chart a smooth course between ire and irie. With such pleasantness and inclusivity built into the language and culture, it's no wonder so many foreigners have adopted Jamaica as their own. Of course, the country's cheap goods and services also play a role. It's easy to feel at home in a country when you can afford to buy two or three houses.

Sims had roots in Mississippi and grew up in Chicago, but considered himself Jamaican in many ways thanks to his long association with the island. After running a nightclub called Sapphire's in New York City, he got into the music industry after Johnny Nash asked him to promote a Caribbean concert tour. Sims went on to manage tours for such mainstream pop acts as Paul Anka, Patti LaBelle, Sammy Davis Jr., and Brook Benton. He decided to settle part-time in Jamaica. Sims and Nash bought a house in the upscale neighborhood of Russell Heights. At Nash's request, Bob met Sims there the day after the grounation. He arrived with Planno, Rita, and a guitar. "Bob didn't have dreadlocks at that time," Sims recounts. "Mortimer's dreads were down his back—he looked like a guy from space. Mortimer was like the manager. He did the talking; all Bob did is smile."

Bob actually did more than smile. With Rita providing backup vocals and Bob playing acoustic guitar, he sang some thirty songs for Sims. He was a human jukebox, running through his best work so far. He sang "Bend Down Low," "Stir It Up," "Nice Time," and "Guava Jelly." He didn't want to lose Sims's attention, so he offered up a kind of condensed *Reader's Digest* version of his songs: he played the verse, the chorus, and the hook for each number and then moved on to the next one. Sims was stunned.

Every song he heard sounded like a hit. He loved the rough quality of Rita's voice and how it perfectly supported Bob's. He also admired Bob's presentation. He moved as he sang, swimming in his own music. After Bob finished, Planno told Sims it was important to them that Bob sign with a black company. "Bob had an R-and-B type of presentation," Sims remembers. "You could understand his English. And that was good for us. Because most of the stuff that we had heard, we didn't understand the patois. But Bob didn't sing with that kind of an accent. He had a style that was more American, and we thought that he'd be very easy to break in America." Sims would sign the Wailers to a contract paying them two hundred pounds a week. That was more than Bob had earned from Coxson in a year.

Sims invited Bob to come back the next day to have breakfast. He soon got a lesson on the Jamaican caste system. His Jamaican cook refused to serve Bob. When Sims confronted her, she said she would not serve a Rasta. Sims fired her. But when he hired a replacement, the same thing happened. The man was happy to have the job, but drew the line at cooking food for Rastas. It was beneath him. Sims was startled and confused. Part of what had attracted him to Jamaica was that it was an island of black people. He had tired of all the racial divisions in America—it was the late 1960s and the civil-rights struggle and the black power movement were in full gear. Sims found it disturbing that one group of poor black Jamaicans would discriminate against another group of poor black Jamaicans. In the end, Planno provided him with a Rasta cook. The new chef's recipes often included chopping up fresh ganja and tossing it into whatever he was preparing. His tenure was a long and popular one.

The Rastas' veneration of ganja came as a surprise to Sims. Spiritual highs and pharmacological highs seemed mutually exclusive things. Smoking weed to get close to God seemed as sacrilegious as shooting up in the pews. Before he met Bob, Sims didn't even know what a Rasta was. He had seen them on the street in Kingston, but hadn't identified them in his mind as a separate group, much less as followers of a particular religion. He got a quick education on Rasta ways. "Johnny Nash and I didn't smoke weed at that time," Sims confides. "That was, to us, just not progressive to be high. To look at all the people around us with all the drugs in America, that was not the way to go for business-people."

Sims and Nash's ganja virginity ended when the two Americans paid a visit to Planno's place. Planno lived outside of Kingston. Sims, despite his roots in the South, had never seen such poverty. The houses looked like cardboard boxes. Some of them actually were cardboard boxes. Finally they arrived at Planno's home. It was far from a palace. One of the biggest pieces of furniture was for smoking marijuana. It was a huge pipe—the Rastas called it a chalice—which held several pounds of weed at a time. With its tubes and bubbling whatnots, it looked less like a drug delivery system than a contraption out of a Dr. Seuss book. Planno grabbed a copy of a religious book and began to lecture the many Rastas who had crowded into his house. When his sermon was over, the Dr. Seuss chalice was passed around. Finally it reached Sims and Nash, the ganja neophytes. "The difficulty was, I didn't even smoke cigarettes," recalls Sims. Sucking on the chalice was like putting your mouth around a chimney. When people took a hit, smoke seemed to come from everywhere—nose, mouth, even their ears. Sims and Nash decided to join in. They were ganja virgins no more. Sims fell asleep among the Rastas.

Marijuana has many names in Jamaica. One reason for this is the number of varieties—there are hundreds of them. Another reason is the Man—if you are smoking something illegal, it is best not to let law enforcement know what you are talking about. So marijuana is called wisdom weed, tampee, kiki, kali, kaya, high grade, I-lley, the I-cient tree, and many other things, including, most commonly, ganja. *Cannabis sativa* was given its scientific name by the Swedish botanist Linnaeus in 1753. The plant first came to Jamaica in appreciable amounts during the eighteenth century. It was likely brought over by indentured Indian servants. In 1894, a British commission studied the effects of ganja on the Indian population. The study concluded that there was no reason to ban the plant. The report said: "The fact that many witnesses testified to the peaceable and orderly character that is exhibited in the consumption of ganja goes far to prove that these drugs do not tend to evince crimes of violence."

The Rastafari movement helped spread ganja use, and vice versa. It's hard to get kids into church with promises of stale bread and grape juice; it's considerably easier to get youth interested in religious services that end with everyone getting baked. Up until 1930, ganja was grown mainly in two adjoining parishes, St. Thomas and St. Mary, both home to large numbers of Indians. After 1930, authorities began to find ganja being grown all around the island. A 1935 report from the Jamaican Central Board of Health found that the use of ganja was spreading and that "more than three times as many Jamaicans as East Indians" were using it. The report contained the following fictional exchange between "John Brown" and "Mary Brown." The dialogue was meant to represent the views of ordinary black Jamaicans. It was clearly not meant to evoke Eugene O'Neill.

Mary: John Brown, you are certainly one to worry about nothing at all. Here you look solemn and depressed and have me worried to death. And all because a couple of Coolie boys been smoking ganja!

John: But they are not Indian boys! They are Jamaicans and the sons of respectable, law-abiding folks—just like us.

Garvey and his followers took note. An editorial titled "The Dangerous Weed" appeared in his *New Jamaican* on August 13, 1932, and read (perhaps predictably, given the headline): "Ganja is a dangerous weed. It has been pronounced so by responsible authorities. The smoking of it does a great deal of harm or injury to the smoker; we understand it has the same effect on the subject as opium has . . . Between ganja and fanatical religion, we are developing a large population of half-crazy people who may not only injure themselves, but injure us." But weed was seductive. Some experts report Garvey himself was a marijuana smoker.

Other Jamaican newspapers also condemned the spread of ganja. An editorial by Vere Johns in the *Daily Gleaner* on Monday, June 4, 1951, contended that "the habit is growing amongst all classes and the apathetic attitude of the government and police tend to make our dope peddlers bolder and inclined to increase their activity . . . Repeatedly, I have heard ugly rumours (which ring awfully true) casting a grave doubt in my mind as to what becomes of the huge quantities of ganja periodically seized by the police and presented in Court as exhibits. These are supposed to be destroyed by fire afterwards. But are they really?" Jamaican law enforcement may have been destroying the dope by fire, just as they said. But they may have been doing it one spliff at a time.

While the allure of weed is undeniable, Rastas take the attraction a few steps further and consider it a sacrament. This prayer is said by some Rastas before smoking ganja: "Glory be to the Father and to the maker of creation. As it was in the beginning is now and ever shall be World without end: Jah Rastafari: Eternal God Selassie I." Rasta lore has it that references to ganja were secretly removed from the Bible by mistranslations. Rasta teachings hold that the Bible once read that King Solomon's robes were made from hemp and that the original Hebrews—who, according to the Rastas, were black, yet another fact Babylon doesn't want you to know about—used wisdom weed as incense. Bob argued that "herb is not a drug. Herb is a plant that grow. And God made it so that mankind can take it." Rastas cite several biblical passages to back up their position. Genesis 3:16 reads: "The earth brought forth grass and herb yielding seed after its kind . . . and God saw that it was good . . . And God said, behold, I have given you every herb bearing seed which is upon the face of the earth, and every tree, which is the fruit of a tree yielding seed, to you it shall be meat." And Exodus 10:12 declares: "Eat every herb of the land." It should be pointed out that if you're itching to smoke weed, almost any passage in the Bible can be used to justify firing up a fat blunt, starting with "Let there be light."

Nonetheless, many Rastas believe wholeheartedly that the use of herb is a key to world peace and understanding. Many Jamaicans—Rastas and non-Rastas—say that making fun of herb as a sacrament is a cheap shot. They contend that numerous other religions have employed drugs and alcohol in their spiritual practices, from the use of peyote in worship by some Native Americans to Christian altar wine. Bob reasoned: "Now, herb is the healing of the nation. Going through all of this alien education that everybody's mind is being programmed, the only way some of us can get away from it is through meditation. The only way you can meditate in a place full of confusion is by using herb. So when you smoke the herb, you can meditate through a lot of traffic, a lot of noise, a lot of this." To which many Rastas would add, Amen.

Johnny Nash and Danny Sims launched a new record company called JAD. (The name stood for Johnny and Danny.) Sims focused on recording Bob and bringing him to a worldwide audience. He felt he had to tailor Bob's regional reggae sound to make it fit in on U.S. and U.K. playlists. Sims wasn't running a charity; he wanted to make money. And he wasn't interested in marketing Bob in Jamaica. He felt the music industry there was too corrupt and it was too hard to earn money. He brought in Jimmy Norman, a songwriter, a performer, and a member of the American pop group the Coasters, to work with the Wailers. He also hired Arthur Jenkins, another American songwriter, to work on the group's arrangements. He brought in studio musicians such as the South African trumpeter Hugh Masekela to assist in broadening the Wailers' appeal.

Ganja became a staple at Sims's Russell Heights pad. It was as commonplace as condiments at other houses. It was passed around as casually as a saltshaker. It was smoked in the morning as a wake-me-up, in the afternoon to pass the day, and at night to wind down. Water from the ganja pipes stained the rugs and proved impossible to get out. Dozens of Rastas—some there to play music, others there to listen, one and all there to smoke weed—came in and out of the house every day. Neighbors began to complain. They began to grumble about "the American troublemakers." Some neighbors were invited over for a smoke. They stopped grumbling. The ones who were left out complained even louder. It's hard not to feel low when everyone else is getting high. Sims wondered what all the fuss was about. "The houses were far apart, it wasn't like the guy next door could smell what was going on," he notes. "They only could guess what was going on." Of course, the neighbors' guesses were usually right—more smoke was pouring out of the house than from the Vatican after the election of a new pope.

Still, there was actual work being produced. Sims was impressed by the work ethic of the core group of Wailers: Bob, Bunny, and Peter. It was even more noteworthy given the prodigious amount of ganja the trio was smoking. "The three of those guys never came late," Sims says, marveling. "Everyone else around them never showed up except late. There was no such thing in Jamaica as people showing up on time. It was unusual because Bob, Peter, and Bunny always were on time."

But despite the hard work, the good times, and all the smoke, Bunny was growing frustrated with the advice of the American arranger, Jenkins, and the American songwriter, Norman. Meanwhile, Nash was rearranging some of the Wailers material for his own voice so he could record some of it for his next album. If the Wailers' stuff was good enough for Nash, Bunny wondered, why were all these Americans trying to tell the Wailers how to be musicians? The Americans kept offering unsolicited advice to the Wailers on how to write, how to arrange, how to sing, how to harmonize. The drill went on for weeks. Bunny grew angrier. He wasn't happy with Sims's ideas for the group. "Johnny Nash wasn't altering or changing his voice to sing Bob's songs, but it was working," fumes Bunny. "And Johnny Nash, in reality, sounded very much like Johnny Mathis, when Bob only sounded like Bob. If I was made to choose in a purchase of both artists, I would take Bob Marley—even if he was talking."

Parties were a regular occurrence at Sims's house. At a get-together in 1967, one of the attendees was Cindy Breakspeare, who would go on to win the Miss World contest in later years. At the time of the party, she was around thirteen years old. It was late at night and Sims came over to Cindy and pointed out one of his other guests. Sims remarked: "Oh, do you know who that is? That's Bob Marley and he's gonna be a big star one day." Cindy said she didn't even remember the meeting and that Bob made no impression on her. Another guest at the party says that Cindy, who was from an upper-middle-class family, was horrified that there were Rastas at the party. Cindy recalled later: "He was just passing through and we were just kids hanging out."

Stop. Fast-forward. Sometimes you have to skip ahead to understand the course of events. Cindy may have been the love of Bob's life—if you ask her. She may have also been the greatest mistake of Bob's life—if you ask his wife, Rita. Bob's affair with Cindy blossomed after he was a star. But they first encountered each other when he was struggling to make it. She was, after Rita, his greatest muse, inspiring some of his most tender songwriting. Her influence also provoked a militant creative backlash in Bob. His relationship with Cindy helps you understand how he related to women and how women related to him. It illustrates how, in a few short years, perceptions of Rastas changed. They went from outcasts to insiders, from the scorned to the desired. A Rasta who was once ignored by a great beauty, after things changed, could go on to bed Miss World.

Cindy was born on October 24, 1954, in Toronto, Canada. Her mother was a homemaker and her father was in the insurance business. Her father was a white Jamaican and her mother was black, but Cindy holds that "neither of my parents appears black just to look at them." Cindy moved to Jamaica when she was four years old and attended Immaculate Conception Academy in Kingston. She grew up knowing little about Rastafari. "We were not aware of it as a religious movement," Cindy confesses. "I used to walk home from school every day from the back gate of Immaculate, and if you saw a Rasta on the street, you would keep your head straight and hope that he didn't say anything to you. Because they were all crazy—they smoked ganja and they basically were all crazy. That kind of was the thinking at that time."

Cindy's parents divorced when she was about seven years old. She grew into a rebellious girl who moved away from her mother around the age of seventeen. She wanted to travel the world and learn about other people and places. Cindy says she first really became aware of Bob Marley in 1973 after the release of *Catch a Fire*. She was living in Kingston when her brother, Stephen, brought home a copy of the album. There were only two records she really listened to that year, *Catch a Fire* and Marvin Gaye's *What's Going On*. The two alternated on her turntable and every other album faded into the background. Cindy had listened to reggae, but nothing had excited her like Bob's music. She explains the attraction this way: "Well, first of all that guitar solo at the beginning of 'Concrete Jungle.' We had never heard anything like that in reggae music before. It was like 'Wow, what is this?' It was just exciting and different. You just had to hear it over and over again. So of course we did listen to it over and over again. And the whole album just proved to be really thrilling."

She later saw Bob open up for Marvin Gaye at the Carib Theatre in Kingston. "And at that point I wouldn't even tell you that I remembered meeting Bob up at Danny's," Cindy notes. "Seeing Danny again and people saying 'Remember that night?' 'Oh yes. It was you?' It was that sort of thing. I didn't even remember it then."

Her relationship with Bob would soon become unforgettable.

By 1971—two years before Bob would seduce a starstruck Cindy—Sims had made little progress in breaking the Wailers' music abroad. He took copies of Bob's single "Bend Down Low" to American deejays and was turned away. Radio programmers didn't understand the beat and couldn't make out the lyrics. One American deejay told Sims: "You bring your guns, you bring your dope, you bring your money, but you're not gonna get this record played here. And secondly, Danny, go find yourself a translator."

Later in that same year, another business opportunity came up. Johnny Nash had been hired to star in a movie in Sweden called

Vill så gärna tro (*I Want to Believe*). The movie was produced and written by Gunnar Hoglund. It was the story of a black American jazz-ballet teacher (played by Nash) who romances a Swedish stewardess (played by Christina Schollin, who would later become world famous as the star of Ingmar Bergman's *Fanny and Alexander*). The film was meant to be topical, controversial, and sexy.

Nash had begun work on the movie in late 1970. The soundtrack was to feature rock and reggae. John "Rabbit" Bundrick, an American keyboard player, had been brought in to write and produce the rock songs. Nash was supposed to compose some reggae songs. Nash had rented a house on Sigurdsvagen, Nockeby, which is about three miles from the heart of Stockholm. Several Swedish musicians were brought in to support the project: guitarist Jan Schaffer, guitarist Bjorn Linder, drummer Ola Brunkert, and bassist Bo Haggstrom. Nash decided it would be best to focus on his acting instead of spending his time teaching Swedish musicians how to play soul and reggae songs. In March 1971, he asked Schaffer to come to his house in Nockeby. He said he wanted to play a tape of a great new singer from Jamaica. The sound of reggae filled the room.

Nash gushed: "Isn't Bob Marley great?"

Schaffer didn't quite understand or appreciate the music. The lyrics were not the only thing requiring translation—the music seemed as if it was in a different language, too. The songs sounded rough to him. And they didn't sound like the smooth reggae he had heard Nash play. But Nash said the man on the tape would be coming in a few days to help him write music for the film.

Bob flew to Stockholm in 1971, leaving his fellow Wailers behind in Jamaica to manage the band's affairs. In the photo on the passport he took with him on the trip, he has a ragged Afro that seems to just be forming into dreadlocks. He arrived in Stockholm wearing a suit. There was a shortage of rooms, so Bob had to sleep in a wardrobe closet. The first time Bundrick met Bob, he was stunned. He didn't think Bob was capable of tuning his guitar properly. And he couldn't understand Bob's Jamaican patois. He thought the whole enterprise was doomed.

Bundrick had problems understanding him, but Bob talked to him more than to the other musicians. He seemed to dislike the Swedes. At one point, one of the Swedish musicians tried to joke around with Bob and asked him to "say something Jamaican." Bob was annoyed and left the room. There was a lot of drinking and cavorting at the house, but Bob was often a bystander. He once said that he would drink "a little wine sometime, that's all. Spirits bad. Why people drink is they want feeling I get when I smoke herb. Everybody need to get high but some people gettin' high with the wrong things. Alcohol wrong. Herb does grow." Bob spent a lot of time in his room, playing his guitar alone. Rabbit recalls him sitting on his bed strumming "Stir It Up." As Rabbit remembers the period: "Bob ate a lot of fish-head soup and stayed in his room a lot smoking pot. I never once saw him drunk. He did drink a drink made out of honey and something, but I don't know what it was. Bob was always cool and didn't let things get on top of him. He seemed to always take life in his stride. Ready to tackle anything that came his way. Bob was a very strong man."

Bob seemed fascinated by the snow. Now and again he would make fish tea and other Jamaican dishes and share them with the musicians. He was annoyed when someone threw out some fish heads he had been saving, thinking they were garbage. When he found out the culprit was Marlene Lingard, Rabbit's Swedish girl-friend, he started sweet-talking instead. When Rabbit was out of hearing range, he would tell her, "Hey, Marlene, when Rabbit, mon, ain't around, why don't we do it, huh?" At one point, when money was running low, Sims brought in an American cardsharp. He figured he would have no problems winning cash from the locals. But a Swedish poker player took Sims's hood for everything he had. A fight erupted, chairs were broken, but nobody touched Bob. He remained cool and calm and told all comers, "Yuh naa rass wit I, mon." Observes Rabbit: "He wasn't afraid of anything or anybody, at least that was the image he projected. I loved the way he stood up for himself, no matter what. He was right and everybody else was wrong. What confidence that guy had."

Bob said little about his life in Jamaica. Rabbit contends: "I must admit, that in all the time I lived with and worked with Bob, that he never mentioned [Bunny and Peter] to me, not once!" Bob also took up with a Swedish woman while he was in Stockholm. "We all did. Bob was no exception. Those were very lonely times for us all," Rabbit discloses. "We were away from home for months on end. A house full of blokes, come on, there's got to be women around. He wasn't the sort who flaunted, or took advantage of it, though. I don't remember her name, but it was nothing serious. Just some company to pass away the days and months." Rabbit said Bob never mentioned Rita or the fact that he was married: "I guess that was private, and nobody else's business. He did like his women, and I guess she was a special one, but maybe not the only one."

Vill så gärna tro premiered on September 4, 1971. Nash and Schollin performed a song from the film called "That's a Daydream I've Got" on the *Hylands Horna* television show, which was the Swedish equivalent of *The Tonight Show*. Local gossip columnists speculated in print that the costars, in a case of life imitating art, had begun an offscreen romance. None of the publicity helped the film at the box office. The critics and the public hated it. It remained in theaters for about a week. The soundtrack was never released. Marley left Sweden.

Despite the failure of the film, Rabbit remembers the whole experience as a good time. "Yes, I saw the film, but Bob wasn't there, as far as I can remember. They were heady days, so it's hard to know for sure. I do know that there was one scene in the film, a party scene, where Nash was wooing 'the Swedish girlfriend' and got up and sang a tune for her, that the director invited all of us, me, Bob, Fred Jordan—our musical director—Danny Sims, and all our girlfriends and friends, to come to the film studio and take part in the filming of the party scene as extras. Bob was there then. We all went. Free party, booze, and women, why not?"

Women in Bob's life were like hotel guests. They never stayed long, and after they left, everything was put back in place just like it had been when they arrived. Stop. Fast-forward. Skip ahead in time. Years after Sweden, Bob would encounter a woman who had a more lasting impact on him than the loves he had drifted through in the past: Cindy Breakspeare. She seemed, at first, to be another of Bob's casual encounters. Along with her brother, she moved into a group house at 56 Hope Road in 1973. She was attracted to the property because it had a "bohemian" feel. There were various artists and musicians living there already.

"We were two kids looking for a flat," Cindy states. "We needed to be somewhere central because we didn't own a car, so central was very important. It doesn't get much more central than Hope Road. So fine, we moved into the place that is now the studio on the ground floor. We had two bedrooms and a bathroom and a kitchen and a dining area, and we just loved it. The vibe was very easygoing, you do what you want, see who you want; it suited us perfectly."

One of the people who was spending time in the house was Bob Marley. She would see him in the hallways, pass by him coming out the front door when she was going in. They never said much more than hello or good-bye. Cindy didn't immediately sense romantic possibilities. " 'Cause Bob had a girlfriend living with him there before," she explains. "First it was Esther Ander-son. And then it was Yvette. I knew them both. And they used to come and go in our place and sit and chat and what have you." Cindy moved out of Hope Road for a time and moved back in 1975. Bob was living there and rehearsing. His ex-girlfriends had moved out or moved on. Cindy now had him all to herself.

Cindy says Bob had a magic quality about him. He was quiet but confident. He radiated a sense of freedom with his hair and his clothing, but he also had a strict code of ethics, and a tight circle of friends. The fact that he was on the rise made him all the more intriguing. "We were very much aware of what was happen-ing with Bob's career, and realized that he was definitely going places and destined to great things," she admits. "We were all big fans by then." Bob would find reasons to stop by and talk to Cindy. Sometimes it was just to say hello. Other times it was to see if she was home. Was she safe? Was she happy? Did she need help with anything? Could he come in? Bob also found a new place to rehearse, conveniently right outside Cindy's room. He would sit outside her door, guitar in hand, and sing songs such as "Turn Your Lights Down Low." If you want to win a woman's heart, why not sing her one of the greatest love songs ever com-posed? Cindy feels he wrote that song with her in mind.

The two began an affair. But they never went on dates. Bob's idea of a date was to show up at Cindy's door with a ripe mango. The fresh-fruit approach might not have worked when he was Bob from Trench Town. It worked now that he was Bob from the Wailers. Cindy freely admits that she wasn't wined and dined: "No, man, it wasn't that type of situation. First of all, he was very absorbed in what he was doing. Very busy all the time, so we basically just hung out at 56 Hope Road and got together in the yard, walked out in the garden, picked a mango, looked at the stars, whatever. A date would have been driving out to go to Port Royal to eat fish. We didn't do dates in the conventional sense of the word."

In 1976, Cindy made history of her own. She wanted to raise money for her education and to travel. She began to compete in fitness and beauty pageants. On August 29, she won the Miss Jamaica Body Beautiful title at the Sheraton Kingston Hotel. (She also was given special notices for best figure and best conditioning.) On September 18, she won the Miss Universe Bikini contest in London, beating out twenty-five other women from thirteen countries. The *Sunday Gleaner* ran her picture on the front page and noted that her measurements were "bust 35 in., waist 24 ½ in. and hips 36 ½ in." And in December, she captured her biggest title: Miss World. Says Cindy: "Jamaicans were thrilled. Very thrilled. At that time the violence in Jamaica had just really started escalating and we were getting a lot of negative publicity about that. And I found that Jamaicans in general were really pleased that here was something that was positive and they could brag about and was a good thing. So generally they were very pleased." After her win, the *Daily Gleaner* exulted on December 5, 1976: "The winning of the title by this Jamaican girl has attracted infinitely more publicity, and stories about her have been given ten times as much prominence in the foreign press than any reports of violence in Jamaica."

But with the title came scrutiny. Cindy's face and figure were splashed across major papers in England, the Caribbean, and the United States. There were some critics who argued that she should never have been in the contest. In 1975, the Jamaican government had decided not to enter Miss World because the apartheid state of South Africa was participating. Cindy told papers that she would have withdrawn if government officials had contacted her. She was "strongly" against apartheid, but noted that

South Africa had sent one black contestant and one white one and had promised to make future selections multiracial. "It was certainly never my intention to go against the wishes of the government," she was quoted as saying at the time. "As far as I was concerned it was part of a personal plan to try to get somewhere in life."

Journalists were now asking questions about her relationship with Bob. The *Sun* asked, "Will Miss World Marry the Prince of Wails?" In Jamaica, there was an uproar over the relationship, which had avoided the spotlight before Cindy's Miss World title. Cindy laments: "The upper echelon of society were outraged because they didn't know much about Rasta then, and as far as they were concerned, who is this dirty little dreadlocks boy? The rumors that used to circulate were outrageous, you wouldn't believe them. That Rastas don't wash their hair, or all kinds of insects crawling in it. You name it, they were saying it."

Bob's Rasta brethren weren't happy about the affair either. Cindy was light, bright, and damn near white. She was parading around on stages in bathing suits when the Rasta brethren would have preferred her to be home with her pretty head wrapped up, her ample bust covered, and her shapely legs hidden behind a long skirt. What was Bob doing with such a scandalous woman? How could he have brought her into the community? And why couldn't he have found some girls just like her for all of them?

Bob was also a married man. Rita knew about Cindy and didn't care for her. She didn't even like her name and pronounced it Cin-dy—accent on the "sin." When Rita went shopping, Bob would sometimes ask her to pick up a few things for Cindy. Rita would hold her tongue and get the items. She figured she was the real wife and Cindy was just a passing rain. Cindy says Bob's marriage never figured into their affair. She contends, "By then, y'know, Bob was living at Hope Road, and [Rita] was still living at Bull Bay and they were pretty much, I guess you would say, separated for want of a different word, or that is certainly the impression he gave and how it looked to all of the rest of us." It wouldn't be the first time, or the last, that a married man gave his mistress the impression, true or not, that his marriage was all but over.

The press and public saw Bob and Cindy as opposites. Behind the doors of 56 Hope Road, the reality was something different. "The truth is we had a lot in common," Cindy asserts. "I loved music. I've always loved music. That was something I was always drawn to. And we both had a love of physical culture, because I was a gym enthusiast. That's how I got into competitions in the first place. The first two I won were bodybuilding contests. By then, we were both into our vegetarian diets. Very much into taking care of the body and what you put in it. So we really had a lot in common. Even though we were from two different echelons of the society, we were on the same path. And you can't beat the appeal of wanting what you're not supposed to have."

On July 21, 1978, Cindy sparked another controversy by giving birth to a son by Bob. His name was Damian. Cindy laughs as she says: "There was the usual outrage coming from polite society. 'She's doing what now?' I had girlfriends whose parents sat them down and said, 'You see what Cindy Breakspeare has done? Don't even think about it.' "

Over the years, Bob had children by several different women outside of his marriage to Rita. "How many kids do you have?" Marley was asked in 1979. "Not plenty" was his cagey reply. Despite having different mothers, Bob's acknowledged sons and daughters often lived together. Cedella, Bob's eldest daughter with Rita, reveals: "That had a lot to do with my mom and my dad. When me and my mom we talk, we talk like woman-to-woman stuff. I'm like, 'Mom, I don't know how you did it.' I love all my brothers and sisters equally—it's not like I love the three that my mom had with my dad more than I love Damian [Cindy's son] and Julian [born to Lucy Pounder in 1975]. It's the same love. They've been in our lives all of their lives. He kind of forced them on us. I remember him and Rohan. He dropped Rohan [born to Janet Hunt in 1972] off one night and said, 'Rohan is coming to live with you now.' Rohan's mother showed up when Dad was gone and she kind of forced her way in and kind of took him. And we were all going like, 'Oh sh--, how are we going to tell Daddy that this woman came and took Rohan?' Because he really wanted us all to live together."

Cindy continued to have an impact on Bob's songwriting. In addition to "Turn Your Lights Down Low," she may have inspired the romantic mood on the album *Kaya*. "There are many songs on that famous one full of love songs that are attributed to me," she purrs. "Who knows? It was what was happening in our lives at the time." After *Kaya*'s release, Bob talked to her about some of the songs.

"Y'see you made me write all these love songs," said Bob. "And they're saying now, I've gotten soft."

Bob's next album after *Kaya* would be the more militant *Survival*. That album would not contain a single love song.

Six years before *Kaya* and his shift in tone, however, Bob was still looking for an international hit. Sims was still eager to break him to the global audience. In 1972, he decided to take the Wailers to England. Johnny Nash was readying an album and a tour and he wanted the Wailers' support. Bunny was put off from the beginning. Bunny claims that "their first move, when we arrived in London, was to take from us our passports for the processing of our work visas." He felt the move was aimed at controlling the band, since they would be stranded without their passports. But the Wailers were pleased with the flat that Sims had rented for them in an upscale area of London. The house was stocked with food and within walking distance of stores. There was a huge park across the street where the Wailers could go to play soccer and relax. And, in something that seemed like a sign from above to the group, the rehearsal studio that had been picked out for them was located in an area called Kingston. Fortune's frown had finally turned into a grin.

Sims had signed Nash and Bob to CBS Records as a package deal. It was the kind of deal Bob had hoped for. CBS was committed to putting out an album of his material outside of Jamaica. But Sims had a big hurdle to jump. Nobody outside of Jamaica knew who Bob Marley was. And many of them didn't care to know. Then Sims had a brainstorm. Kids were the ones buying most of the pop records. Why not reach out to kids directly?

To promote his stars, he booked Nash and Bob to play in several hundred high schools around England. The pair would play two shows in the morning and two shows in the afternoon. Bob would open for Nash, accompanying him on acoustic guitar. Then Bob would play backup for Nash. "It was the kids getting a chance to get out of school, and for a break," Sims explains. "They would call an assembly, they'd go into the auditorium, and we'd do a show. Johnny did half an hour and Bob did half an hour." The two performers received little compensation for the tour. Sims wanted to boost their recognition among the record-buying public in advance of their albums' release. It worked. Soon after the tour kicked off, word spread, and when Nash and Bob showed up at schools, there were long lines of youngsters waiting for their arrival.

But the Nash-Marley collaboration had its detractors—namely, the other Wailers. Nash had put together a backing band called the Sons of the Jungle. When the Wailers saw his tour bus, they were offended. The side of the bus read JOHNNY NASH AND THE

SONS OF THE JUNGLE KINGS OF REGGAE TOUR. To the Wailers, this was wrong for all sorts of reasons. The name seemed to imply that reggae was jungle music. And it also declared that Nash and his bunch were the kings of the genre. The Wailers were determined to disprove that.

Bob had been joined by Bunny, Peter, and Family Man for a larger tour that would branch out beyond high schools. Members of the Cimaroons, a Jamaican band in London, were invited to help support the Wailers. They rehearsed long hours. But for most of the tour, the rest of the Wailers had to watch Bob and Nash from the audience. According to Bunny, Sims said that their work visas had yet to come through. Near the end of the tour, the group decided to play for free, simply so they could go onstage without waiting for the paperwork to be processed.

The Wailers were determined to show Sims and Nash and all the Americans what they had been missing. They wanted to let the so-called Kings of Reggae know who really deserved the throne. The concert took place at a seaport town in the northeast of Britain. The population of the town was 100 percent white. Nobody had heard of reggae, much less Bob Marley. The Wailers saw this as a welcome challenge. They had been trained. They had the songs. They had the skills. They felt they would win over any crowd.

Bunny peeked out into the audience before the show began. "As far as I can recall, there might have been only one dark-skinned girl visible, and visible she was," he recalls. The Wailers took their places onstage. They had some early problems. First, Family Man's bass was untuned. And then Bob's guitar strap broke. The Wailers were looking less like kings and more like jokers. But the band quickly put the early stumbles behind them.

The Wailers tore through their best songs, including "Duppy Conqueror," "Small Axe," and "Keep on Moving." That last song they stretched out for fifteen minutes as the crowd spontaneously formed an enormous line and paraded through the venue, kicking and shouting. "It reminded us of the Israelites circling the walls of Jericho," Bunny remembers. The band moved on to "Lively Up Yourself" and "Soul Rebel." The audience loved it. They threw tokens of their adulation on the stage: cups, handkerchiefs, hats, and other articles. Bunny claims he even saw a police cap.

It was clear to everyone in the audience: the Wailers were the true Kings of Reggae. "After that show, everybody came out and all they were talking about, Who's that group? Who opened for Johnny Nash? It was different vibration, you hear?" Family Man says, laughing.

But the charts would tell a different story. Johnny Nash's album *I Can See Clearly Now*, which featured several songs written by Bob Marley, was released in 1972. It was an international smash. The title track was a Top Ten hit around the world. Nash's versions of Bob's songs "Stir it Up" and "Guava Jelly" also received heavy radio airplay. By contrast, Bob's debut single for CBS, "Reggae on Broadway," was a flop. "I think that Bob did feel that the A and R [talent development] people at CBS slighted him," Sims concedes. "You never know with hit records. I felt that 'Reggae on Broadway' was a very good record." Bob came to understand that success on the world stage took more than he'd thought. Said Bob: "You go to England, you think you're Jackson 5. It didn't work like that."

Bob and Nash got along professionally, but Bob never really thought the American singer understood his work. "He's a hard worker, but he didn't know my music," he said. "I don't want to put him down, but reggae really isn't his bag." He would also say of Nash: "He's a nice guy, but he doesn't know what reggae is. He come-a Jamaica, hear a man sing reggae; well, personally him great. But Johnny Nash is not a Rasta; and if you're not a Rasta, you don't know nothin' about reggae."

Bunny said that he and Peter later recovered their passports from the abandoned section of the Home Affairs Office. "Can you imagine that?" Bunny remarked years later. Things were bleak. Friends of the band have said the Wailers were always in the red. And at that point, in that place, Bob, Peter, and Bunny must have been seeing red. The group had been betrayed too many times. They had scored chart-topping singles in Jamaica and made no money. Red. They had launched a hit-producing record label and seen it come to nothing. Red. They had secured American help and an American label and found themselves stranded in Britain without a tour and without prospects. Red, red, red. The Wailers owed more money than they had made and had no reliable way of making more. The future, as far as anyone could see, was cast in crimson. The Wailers needed to part the Red Sea or drown.

Then, on the blue horizon, Bob spotted an island of hope.

400 YEARS

The Wailers had waited long enough.

One major theme of their work had been waiting. From "I'm Still Waiting" to "400 Years" to "Waiting in Vain," many of the songs penned by the group's original members have dealt with the idea of delay. The band had been made to wait many times. They had to stand by at Studio One and watch their songs go up the Jamaican record charts without any corresponding rise in their income levels. They had to watch Jamaican performers of lesser talent like Millie Small garner international attention while they labored in obscurity in Jamaica. They had to watch Jimmy Cliff become a movie star in the reggae-themed film *The Harder They Come* while Bob's efforts at making a movie soundtrack in Sweden came to nothing. And the Wailers had to watch American pop star Johnny Nash score several worldwide hits from an album that borrowed from the reggae genre that the Wailers had helped to found, and featured several songs that Bob had composed. The Wailers wanted to catch fire. They hadn't caught it yet.

There is an attitude of "soon come" that has long held sway in Jamaica. Waiting for someone? Soon come. Delivery due? Soon come. Desperately in need of some task or service or item or favor? Soon come. There is a general expectation that things, whatever they are, will arrive later than scheduled or expected. Showing up early is considered unforgivably eager. Arriving on time often results in a surprised and unprepared host. Making an appearance a few minutes late is just being polite. There is an acceptance that the whole island is running late, that the clock is meaningless, that time is subjective. Everything and everyone can wait. The implication is that nothing is really of much importance and that no one really has anything of significance to do. The Wailers, when it came to their careers, raged against this idea. They wanted things yesterday. They showed up to business meetings on time. They delivered recordings on schedule. They were all business when it came to business. And yet they always seemed to just miss out on opportunities. They were a step slow, no matter how fast they were going. They were invariably left waiting.

"Only ambition and determination make people survive," Peter would say on the "Red X" tapes. "Many I see die because of impatience."

The wait was finally over.

Chris Blackwell's family had come to Jamaica during the 1600s. "They were Portuguese Jews," Blackwell reports. "At that time there was the Spanish Inquisition and the Jews from the Iberian Peninsula scattered into the New World. My family kind of came through Venice, Holland, England, and Jamaica." In Jamaica, they entered the rum and sugar trades. Blackwell was born in England but grew up in Jamaica. He still feels cheated that he was born on the wrong island. Blackwell asserts: "I'm Jamaican, completely. In my heart, I'm Jamaican." He grew up rich and rudderless. His father never really had a profession and his mother didn't work. Blackwell's grandmother didn't want her grandson to work either. She felt that he should take full advantage of the family's wealth and drift around the world. Blackwell's grandmother had a strong sense of the family's social position. She held firm against certain things. She was against getting one's hands dirty in something as vulgar as employment, and she was against mixed-race dining. Blackwell fancied himself a rebel and a businessman from an early age. He attended Harrow, a private school in London, and sold his fellow students liquor and cigarettes. He was caned in front of the whole school. Then he was expelled. At that point, he was ready to go. It's hard to play the rebel entrepreneur after all your class-mates have seen your bare behind and watched you cry.

Blackwell started his own record label in Jamaica in 1959. He named the venture Island Records after the Alec Waugh novel *Island in the Sun*. The label specialized in Caribbean music. The first record the fledgling company released was a jazz album by Bermudan pianist Lance Haywood. In early 1962, Blackwell returned to England to oversee the company from there. He decided that rather than compete with all the independent producers who had flooded the business—like Coxson Dodd and Duke Reid—he would be better off striking deals with them and selling their wares abroad. Blackwell claims the escalating violence in the sound-system scene didn't drive him off, but the fact that many of his competitors carried firearms wasn't something that would have encouraged him to remain. He explains his departure this way: "When the independents came in 1962, by that time I was selling more records in England than I was in Jamaica. It just seemed to me that Jamaica was going to come very much into its own at that time. And I thought I'd be better off going to England and starting the company there."

For years, Blackwell's career had been almost invisibly intertwined with Marley's. In 1962, Island released Marley's very first single in the U.K. Recalls Blackwell: "I'd get tapes from Jamaica. This one had 'One Cup of Coffee' on one side and 'Judge Not' was on the other side. It was by Robert Morley. The reason I remember it was Robert Morley is because at that time there was a very successful British actor, a very foppish, jowly-type actor, with that same name. I thought the name was so funny compared to the music. So I put out the first record in England by Bob Marley under the name of Robert Morley."

Blackwell's first big international hit was Millie Small's ska-pop "My Boy Lollipop" in 1964, which sold more than six million copies and helped popularize ska around the world. Blackwell went out on tour with Small, traveling around the Caribbean and to Europe and America. He realized there were many more markets for his music. He began to think bigger. "I was suddenly catapulted out of purely Jamaican music into pop music," he remembers. "Which I never was up until that time. And then from that into rock music." He brought Free, Cat Stevens, and King Crimson onto the label. He thought there were interesting things happening in British rock and committed himself entirely to the scene. He signed bands based on whether he liked the music, not on whether he thought it might be an instant bestseller. He wanted career artists. He brought Steve Winwood to Island. He passed on Pink Floyd. An assistant told him he was making a mistake and that Pink Floyd would sell millions of records. Blackwell replied: "Not on Island they won't."

In the early 1970s, Blackwell revisited the Jamaican music scene. He began managing the career of Jimmy Cliff, whom he thought had superstar potential. Cliff won the lead role in the movie *The Harder They Come*, which became an international smash in 1972. Directed and cowritten by Jamaican filmmaker Perry Henzell, *The Harder They Come* told the story of a Jamaican man's struggle to become a recording star. Cliff's character, Ivan (who wears a shirt emblazoned with an iconic star), gets caught up in the guns and ganja culture of Trench Town. Ivan's best friend in the film is a Rasta, and his worst enemy is a rapacious music producer. Ivan is paid twenty dollars for his first record. Many Jamaican musicians could see their lives reflected in the film—including all of the Wailers. Island released the soundtrack and Blackwell helped produce the film. Cliff had a small following in Europe thanks to a few moderately successful singles, including "Wonderful World (Beautiful People)." But *The Harder They Come* made him a celebrity. His songs on the soundtrack, such as "Many Rivers to Cross," became anthems.

The premiere of *The Harder They Come* at the Carib Theatre in Kingston was a wild affair. The theater held fifteen hundred people. It was filled up, and there was a line outside so long, customers at the front couldn't see the end of it. The movie played to packed houses in Kingston for months. Jamaicans had long appeared on the margins of films, like the James Bond thriller *Dr. No*. In Henzell's vision, black Jamaicans were finally the leads. The film was featured at festivals around Europe and won the Best Young Cinema Award at the 1972 Venice Film Festival. It also played for years at theaters in college towns around the United States. Henzell had done what the Jamaican music industry had been trying to do for decades—he had introduced reggae culture to the globe.

Henzell had met Bob Marley in 1968. "I first ran into him when I was doing research for *The Harder They Come*," he recounts. "I was meeting with Mortimer Planno, who was living down in Trench Town. Bob was a youngster in those days; he used to come around Mortimer Planno—I don't know, for spiritual guidance or something . . . But that's when I first ran into him. He didn't have locks at the time. As far as I was concerned, he was a youngster like any other musician in Trench Town." Henzell never considered using the Wailers' music on the soundtrack. "They hadn't really broken through yet. I wasn't that much aware of them. They weren't really a force. They didn't catch my attention until after the film had been finished."

Toots Hibbert was featured on the soundtrack and it helped win him a larger fan base. "The first time I saw [the film], I saw it at a place called the Carib Theatre at Crossroads at Kingston, Jamaica," Toots reports. "I was just glad to see that I was in the film. I didn't know how to feel at the time—I just feel excited. It was like nothing I had ever seen before." Henzell's film mixed the real and the surreal, connecting the hardscrabble Jamaican music industry with scenes of Wild West–inspired gunplay. Reggae had a sound, and now it had a look. Reggae seemed ready to break, and Cliff was positioned to become a superstar. Then, in 1972, Cliff told Blackwell he was leaving the label.

Blackwell remembers events this way: "By that time, I was almost entirely engrossed in rock. The only person I had been working with really in Jamaican music at that time was Jimmy Cliff, and the week before I met Bob Marley, Jimmy Cliff had left Island, which was devastating to me. Because I was very tight with him, I put a lot of energy, love, and everything into it. And he left. He left because he felt I hadn't really done for him as much as I said I would do. He hadn't earned as much as I'd told him he would earn. He was offered a deal by EMI and he took it. Moved on. I can understand it from his point of view. But I was devastated by it. Because I knew exactly how to break reggae at that time. I knew exactly how to break Jimmy Cliff at that time. The next record, I was going to have him in the T-shirt he was in in *The Harder They Come* and promote him as that. Because the people who were interested in that music were white college kids and Jamaicans. So Jimmy Cliff leaves, I'm devastated by it."

In music, the biggest sounds have come from the smallest labels. When Columbia Records was a fledgling label in the 1930s, it helped give birth to the blues by putting out records by artists such as Bessie Smith. A host of other independent labels, such as Okeh, Paramount, Vocalion, and Black Swan, helped popularize the genre. In the 1950s, Sun Records helped launch the careers of Ike Turner, Elvis Presley, and Jerry Lee Lewis and was a key player in bringing rock and roll to the mainstream. In the 1980s, small labels like Sugar Hill and Def Jam put rap on the cultural map before the big corporations discovered the sound. In the 1990s, the Seattle-based indie label Sub Pop released Nirvana's first album and championed alternative rock. In the 1970s, Blackwell's Island Records was the innovative independent of note. The music industry followed.

Island Records was located in a London church. It was fitting, because Bunny liked to jokingly refer to Blackwell as the Lord. He found the reverence some people in the music industry had for Blackwell amusing. "The name Blackwell was a known name to the Wailers. But when mentioned by anyone, including Coxson, it was as if they were relating to the Lord," he cracks. Blackwell had bought the church in the 1960s and converted it into a temple of music. The Island offices were at one end, there were recording studios in the middle, and Blackwell's apartment was at the other end. The company was Blackwell's life. It was where he worked and slept. It was his personal house of worship. And on the day the Wailers arrived there, his prayers—and the Wailers'—would be answered.

The week before the Wailers arrived at his office, Blackwell had gotten a call from Brent Clarke, a music publicist. "I didn't even know him that well," said Blackwell. "He just rang me and said, 'Oh, by the way, Bob Marley and the Wailers are in town. Are you interested?' " Clarke had been working for Johnny Nash. He had been charged with promoting Nash's "I Can See Clearly Now." He had overheard a conversation at Island in which the Wailers' name had come up. He mentioned the incident to Family Man, who asked Clarke to set up an interview between the Wailers and Island. Clarke begged off at first, since he was there to promote "I Can See Clearly Now," not the Wailers. Family Man told him, "I can see clearly now that the Wailers need this meeting." Clarke agreed to make a call.

Blackwell had heard stories about the Wailers. Most of them were negative. They had a bad reputation, in part because they'd had the temerity to start their own label. The bosses of the Jamaican music industry didn't want them to succeed and had an interest in trashing their reputation. "I kind of heard vaguely about them," recalls Blackwell. "I'd heard that the general reputation about them was they were unruly people, difficult to deal with— impossible to deal with, in fact. Dishonorable." But the fact that the Wailers had challenged their local record industry, though it turned off other producers, intrigued Blackwell. He was looking for artists who were willing to upend tradition. To Blackwell, it was a sign that the Wailers had drive. He could respect that. Ambition was a component of success. He had started Island with a thousand-dollar investment. He was a big tree now, but he had started out a small ax.

Island Records was well named. The poet John Donne once wrote that "no man is an island," but men and women who come from islands sometimes have a special quality about them. Being bounded by water can limit your vision; it can also focus your ambition. There is a bonding that takes place when people share tight national quarters. It can help to spark a fierce cultural pride. You are reminded of Winston Churchill in World War II crying that "we shall defend our island, whatever the cost may be," and, in a paraphrase of Shakespeare, declaring his country to be "this blessed plot, this realm, this England." Could it be a mere coincidence that two island nations, England and Japan, have come close to ruling the world? Could it be just a quirk of fate that the island of Manhattan—especially if you ask people who live there—is arguably the center of American cultural life? Blackwell, like Bob, was an island man. He had lived his life on two islands— England and Jamaica. He respected self-sufficiency, the ability to float serenely in a sea of troubles. Donne done got it wrong. Some men *are* islands. Blackwell could see in Bob the future of Jamaican music.

Blackwell developed a new opinion of the Wailers the moment he saw them. It was a time before the age of video channels. People heard bands on record or on eight-track but they didn't always know what they looked like or how they moved. Blackwell was looking upon Bob, Peter, and Bunny for the first time. They were dressed casually. They weren't extravagant in their manner. But there was a power that emanated from them. Gushes Blackwell: "It was like the real character from *The Harder They Come* walking in the office. The real revolutionary-type characters."

By then, Blackwell knew a bit about why the Wailers were there. They had been stranded in London. The Nash tour was over, Bob's single "Reggae on Broadway" had been a flop, and the band needed money and a new direction. But the Wailers didn't communicate a sense of desperation. They strode into Island as if they owned the place. They were a reggae band, but they were rock stars. Blackwell describes their arrival: "They were charismatic. They were down-and-out. They were busted. Completely busted. And still they walked in the office like they were gods. It was incredible. It's one thing when somebody has a name or a reputation or you read about them or see them on TV, and when they walk in they exude charisma because they've been built up. But when they walk in and they're down-and-out and they exude charisma, that is really something." The Wailers could sense that Blackwell's opinion of them was changing before their eyes. Observes Bunny: "He couldn't hold back his opinion that the Wailers weren't the gangsters and killers that he was made to believe."

The Wailers didn't bring any music to play for Blackwell. This was just a meeting. But it was all Blackwell needed. It was great timing—another component of stardom. He had been filled with anger at the departure of Cliff. The Island Records boss had all this drive, and all these plans, and he didn't know what to do with them. His energy had turned inward and was eating his gut. He was having trouble sleeping and focusing. And now into his office walks a man who embodied the image he wanted to manufacture for Cliff. Bob was the real thing. It was as if Blackwell was screening *The Harder They Come* in his office and Rhygin had stepped off the screen. Bob looked different and he sounded different. He had short locks, which Blackwell thought made him look "incredibly progressive." Toots, Cliff, and Small had all looked traditional. Bob was a new image for Jamaica. His wild hair evoked Jimi Hendrix, Bob Dylan—and Albert Einstein. There was an intelligence and a sex appeal he had, Blackwell thought, that could help his music to reach a wide audience.

Blackwell and the Wailers sat down at a round conference table. The Wailers asked Blackwell whether he was the same Blackwell who had acted as the U.K. distributor for Coxson Dodd. Blackwell answered yes. Bunny remembers him also saying, "And I gave to Coxson, for the Wailers, hundreds of thousands of pounds sterling." The Wailers had never received the money. Remarks Bunny: "We nearly fainted, shocked by this information."

(Blackwell's recollection of the conversation is different. He said years later that from 1962 to at least 1964 he bought Jamaican recordings from Coxson for a flat fee, and so there were no royalties to be shared. And Blackwell doesn't recall any talk of royalties during his first meeting with the group.) Bunny said that the Wailers then asked Blackwell: "Have you ever made sure that Coxson was doing what you thought he should have been doing?" Bunny said that "Blackwell couldn't answer that and showed signs of being interrogated, so we just changed the subject."

Blackwell knew right away that he wanted to make a record with the Wailers. Remembers Blackwell: "I said immediately I'd love to do a deal with them. I asked them how much did they think it would cost to do an album? I explained to them that I think album, I don't really think single, that I think careers. So how much did they think it would cost to record an album, tell me."

Bob told Blackwell that the group could record an album for £4,000. Bob didn't say this next thing, but that was more money than the Wailers had ever spent on an album before. It was almost seventy times the trio's combined weekly salary under Coxson. Blackwell wrote Bob a check right in the office. "And that was it," sums up Blackwell. "We agreed. Right then and there." There was no written contract. Bunny marvels: "[Blackwell] said that he would give us the money and allow us to produce the album ourselves. He mentioned four thousand pounds with which to finance the album. If Chris Blackwell the Lord was willing to trust us, the Wailers, without even a piece of paper signed, then we had to honor the proposal by accepting."

Before Bob left, Blackwell took him aside to have a word. He had never seen the Wailers play. In the rock scene, live performances were important. It was the key to building a devoted audience. Blackwell had just given him a large sum of money. "Were the Wailers any good onstage?" he asked.

Bob replied: "Yeah, mon. We're great."

Was Bob joking or was he that confident? The head of Island Records laughed. He was so taken with his new artist, he was willing to believe just about anything that came from his lips. He shook Bob's hand and told him he would be down in Jamaica in a few months to check on their progress.

The Wailers left the building and soon headed back to Jamaica.

When people around the Island offices heard about the deal, Blackwell says, they laughed at him. They predicted that weeks would go by, and then months, and perhaps years. Jamaican musicians were difficult to deal with and the Wailers were the worst of a bad lot. They would stall and give excuses and the album would never get done. That £4,000 advance was gone. But Blackwell was confident he would not be waiting in vain. Reasons Blackwell: "I knew from past experience that 'difficult to deal with' just meant they wanted to be dealt with fairly. Because in the Jamaican music industry at that time, people weren't dealt with fairly."

So Blackwell settled in and waited for his album. He wouldn't have to wait long.

NO MORE TROUBLE

Very early in Bob Marley's career it was almost too late. The Wailers began recording the songs for *Catch a Fire* in the fall of 1972. Casual fans of reggae think of *Catch a Fire* as the Wailers' debut album. But Bob, Peter, and Bunny, the three original members of the group, were musical veterans. They had been toiling in the Jamaican record industry for ten years. The Wailers had recorded more than two hundred songs. Bob had composed most of them. The band members had performed concerts around Jamaica and the U.K. Bob had worked on a movie soundtrack in Sweden. Although they were old hands in the music scene, they were open to new ways of doing things. They were willing to attempt a sharp stylistic shift in order to court a larger, international audience. They had been around long enough to know they couldn't afford to be delayed much longer. If *Catch a Fire* didn't generate heat, they were finished as a band.

Bob was twenty-seven when the *Catch a Fire* sessions began. Twenty-seven is a tragic age in rock. Janis Joplin, Jimi Hendrix, and Jim Morrison all died at the age of twenty-seven. Kurt Cobain of Nirvana would commit suicide at that same age. Twenty-seven is an age when one is no longer childishly youthful, but one is not yet preoccupied with the ravages of maturity. The graying hair, the thickening gut, the slowing reflexes, the general fading of beauty. Perhaps an awareness of aging arrives around the age of twenty-seven, and that is enough to jolt some artists into drastic life choices. Rock stars who died at twenty-seven seem to have packed an enormous amount of living into their few years, as if they were aware that time was catching up to them. It is difficult to believe, for example, that Hendrix could have recorded all of the songs that he did in the time that he had. It's difficult to believe that bluesman Robert Johnson, who also died at the age of twenty-seven, lived so few years and yet laid so much of the foundation for the way modern rockers would perform—and perish. Bob had lived a full life by twenty-seven. He had several albums, several children, and several extramarital affairs under his sturdy belt. But something else was in store for him instead of musical martyrdom at rock's traditionally appointed hour. The reggae singer Bob Marley would die at age twenty-seven, but he would be reborn—as a rock star.

The primary recording sessions for *Catch a Fire* took place at three facilities in Kingston: Dynamic Studios, Harry J's Studio, and Randy's Studio. Marley would say later that the owners of Dynamic demanded to know how the Wailers had come up with so much money to rent so much studio time. The group began work on the album in October of 1972. They knew exactly what kind of sound they wanted and how to get it. The group's shared Rasta faith gave them a sense of purpose and confidence. Bob, Bunny, Peter, and the Barrett brothers wanted the new collection to reflect their spiritual ideals. It would be reggae. It would be revolutionary. It would be Rasta. Family Man boasts: "We were coming from the song of King David—the chief musician." No other reggae act had released a "concept" album before. Reggae was primarily seen as a genre of novelty singles. The Wailers were attempting something new. Other reggae groups had written short stories. They were writing a novel.

The new album would be a mix of brand-new compositions (such as "Slave Driver" and "No More Trouble") and re-recordings of songs they had previously released for the Jamaican market ("Concrete Jungle," "400 Years," and "Stir It Up"). The tracks selected would be linked in mood and theme. Bunny, Bob, and Peter had all written songs for the new album, but Bob's choices dominated. None of Bunny's songs made the final cut. Peter would have to push Bob hard to have two of his songs—"400 Years" and "Stop That Train"—included. The discussions over which songs to put on the album didn't slow the recording process. The Wailers were used to working quickly and efficiently because studio time was expensive. Most Jamaican musicians were poor. With Blackwell's advance in hand, it seemed they had the funds to work more slowly, if they wanted. Said Bob: "There wasn't really an influence, it was just that this time we got the money from Chris Blackwell to go into the studio and spend as much time as we needed. You see musicians in J.A. have to work to a time limit, so they have to come out of the studio when their time runs out whether they are satisfied or not."

Bob tried to be casual about it, but he did face a deadline. Blackwell was coming to check on the Wailers in a few weeks, and he wanted to be ready. He had to be ready. The album had to be complete. "From what Bob told me, the budget was limited so they didn't have much time," explains Alan "Skill" Cole, a friend of Bob's who also served as the group's manager in the early 1970s. "They had to get their things together and do what they were doing."

Bunny says the primary recording was completed in two weeks. The sessions were run with speed and austerity. Most musicians converse between takes—they talk about work, women, whatever comes to mind. If you listen to the unedited tapes of the Wailers' Jamaican sessions, there is no chatter between songs. No tape was wasted. The focus was on finishing. Time was running out.

Where does inspiration come from? How does a creative spark become a fire? Bob was often guarded about how he created his work. He would turn interviews into mystical sermons, press conferences into panel debates. His media handlers say that they often shied away from setting up formal interviews with him, opting to send journalists over to simply "hang out" with the Wailers and get a general sense of their lifestyle.

When an artist is silent, how do you unlock the secrets of his artistry? Creative people are often reluctant to talk about the origins of their creativity because, in the real world, art is full of compromise, error, and dumb luck. To admit the flaws is to deny its divinity. Plus, inspiration is hard to fathom—hence the many cases of writer's block. It is a process that has long mystified experts, even those who, by their very stature as creative people, would seem most able to decipher the thing that sustains them and informs them. Socrates, in Plato's *Apology*, speaks of conducting this test: "I went to the poets . . . I took them some of the most elaborate passages of their own writings, and asked what was the meaning of them . . . I must say that there is hardly a person present who would not have talked better about their poetry than they did themselves. Then I knew that not by wisdom do poets write poetry, but by a sort of genius and inspiration; they are like diviners and soothsayers who also say many fine things, but do not understand the meaning of them."

When Bunny talks about the *Catch a Fire* sessions, more than three decades after the event, he has wonder in his voice, as if he is amazed to have played a part. Inspiration is an interior process, but great artists often feel as if great work arrives to them from the outside. Bob Dylan has said that his youthful work now mystifies him: "I don't know how I got to write those songs. Those early songs were almost magically written." Friedrich Nietzsche—who once held that "one must have chaos in one, to give birth to a dancing star"—offered up a description of how he was inspired to write *Thus Spake Zarathustra:* "The notion of revelation describes the condition quite simply; by which I mean that something profoundly convulsive and disturbing suddenly becomes visible and audible with definiteness and exactness. One hears—one does not seek; one takes—one does not ask who gives: a thought flashes out like lightning, inevitably without hesitation—I have never had any choice about it." The German philosopher Immanuel Kant explored the question of the origin of inspiration and was baffled. He concluded that the creator of a work of genius "does not know how he came by his ideas" and that the process was "ineffable."

When the Wailers were making *Catch a Fire*, the musicians around them could sense that something important was happening. Marcia Griffiths, who sang backup vocals on several tracks, compared the sessions to a religious experience. Inspiration, though perhaps ineffable, is clearly something palpable. Tchaikovsky, in his letters, wrote, "It would be vain to try to put into words that immeasurable sense of bliss which comes over me directly [when] a new idea awakens in me and begins to assume a definite form. I forget everything and behave like a madman." In another letter, he cautions, "Do not believe those who try to persuade you that composition is only a cold exercise of the intellect. The only music capable of moving and touching us is that which flows from the depths of a composer's soul when he is stirred by inspiration . . . We must be patient, and believe that inspiration will come to those who can master their disinclination."

Bob's lyrics on *Catch a Fire* were worldly and cryptic. He had been listening to Jimi Hendrix, Bob Dylan, and Stevie Wonder. A few months earlier, he had grown a Hendrix-like Afro before letting it lock into dreads. In one interview around this period, Marley quoted specific lyrics from Dylan's "Knocking on Heaven's Door." Marley would later perform alongside Stevie Wonder—who would record "Master Blaster" as a tribute to the reggae great. Marley's songcraft evoked these songwriters, but did not imitate them. Bob once said this about his songwriting process: "Well, the subject come first. Then you have to find ways of explaining it. Sometimes it just come easy. [It depends] on how free your mind can think, really." His new songs had verbal hooks that made them instantly memorable. Phrases like *kinky reggae, catch a fire*, and *stir it up* stuck in the mind like darts on a dartboard. The songs also had a depth that invited repeated listens and deeper scrutiny.

Bob had traveled the world. He had been in America during a period that saw the assassination of Martin Luther King, race riots, Woodstock, and the Vietnam War. With his song "No More Trouble," he announced that his message was now bigger than the cramped streets of Kingston. Bob expounded on "No More Trouble": "It's to the whole world. I don't really bury my mind in Jamaica, you know, I'm talking to the people over the whole world." Griffith remembers that Bob took particular care crafting the background harmonies. He didn't want stiff doo-wops. He wanted to create a backdrop for his sound that was rich, varied, and surprising. He had his singers try out various sounds until he heard something that he felt was unexpected and original.

Another song, "Midnight Ravers," seems to examine the aftermath of the sexual revolution with imagery drawn from the book of Revelations. One can sense the influence of Scratch on this tune. Scratch showed Marley that sex and spirituality were not incompatible. He showed him that listeners embraced songs that they couldn't quite grasp. He showed him how to look for the unseen. He made him a "Duppy Conqueror." "Midnight Ravers" could be set in Kingston or London. The time could be the swinging 1960s or the first days of the Apocalypse. The song could be about straights or gays or something in between. Its tone is not judgmental. In the end, the singer joins in with the "nightlife ravers." Marley said of "Midnight Ravers": "We are midnight ravers, all the sufferers, so please don't let me down, dig!"

The Wailers had worked with a rotating group of musicians throughout their careers. They began as a vocal group. At that point in their professional lives, they were content to use whatever house band was provided by whichever studio they were recording in. The addition of the Barrett brothers as their permanent rhythm section stabilized the group's sound. "I choose the bass, because it is the backbone of the music," Family Man explains. "And my brother Carly choose the drum, which is the heartbeat. If your drummer is not right, then the music gonna have a bad heart. And if the bass is not right, then the music gonna have a bad back. Just imagine the music with a bad back and a bad heart. It would be crippled, you know. So that's where we stand forth and strengthen the music."

Family Man's supple bass lines also supported Bob's vocals and brought out the sweetness in his compositions. Family Man had always wanted to be a vocalist, but understood that he was a far better bassist. His love of singing came out in the way he approached his instrument. Family Man describes his craft: "When I'm playing the bass, I pretend like I am singing baritone. So I play that melodic line so that the lead singer can float, can swing on top of the music, and my brother drop right on the heartbeat. On the one drop—waaah." To emphasize the rhythm section, the Wailers rearranged the studios in which they recorded. The drums were set up in the middle of the room and everything was pointed inward so the bass spilled onto all the sounds they recorded.

Family Man recommended that the group get a man he called his "student," Robbie Shakespeare, to play the bass on two tracks, "Concrete Jungle" and "Stir It Up." Shakespeare was then nineteen years old. He used to live in a house that was known for selling herb in the yard. Family Man was a frequent customer. One day, Shakespeare heard Family Man playing with his band, the Hippy Boys. He was taken by the sound of Family Man's bass.

"Mon, you sound wicked," Shakespeare raved. "You have to teach me how to play."

Family Man replied: "I'm just learning."

"Bwoy, if you just learning, me want to learn wit' you."

Bob went to fetch Shakespeare and brought him to Harry J's. Bunny and Peter were waiting. Shakespeare was tense. The teenage bassist had grown up listening to the Wailers. "All I know is at the time I was saying to myself, sh--, I have to do right. That is my mind. Because with Bob, Peter, and Bunny Wailer, you have to do right." Shakespeare said all three Wailers were running the session on an equal footing. "When the Wailers work in that day, the three of them, the three of them take the lead."

Shakespeare, like his mentor, was a bass player who paid attention to melody. He figured Bob's vocals would tell him what to play on the song. "Concrete Jungle" was a work of urban mysticism. The song has historical scope, linking the chains of slavery to current economic bondage. Visions of the natural world—an unshining sun, a no-longer-playful moon—mix uncomfortably with scenes of urban blight. The images had special resonance for Bob, Bunny, and Peter, who had all left the country for the confines of Kingston. "Skill" Cole says the song wasn't just about Jamaican slums—it also drew on the impressions Bob had gotten of New York City during his trips back and forth to America. The meaning and the melody were important to Shakespeare. "I listen closely to the singer," he says. "I love singing a lot. I listen to the melody and then now I try to play a melodic thing underneath what the singer is singing. Bunny Wailer, which a lot of people don't know, is one of the wickedest bass players that Jamaica have. Bunny Wailer gave me the intro and I come up with the other part."

Months later, Family Man, after a trip abroad, brought a just-off-the-presses copy of *Catch a Fire* to Jamaica.

"There's a track on this album, bwoy, it wicked and I don't know if it I play it or you."

Shakespeare and Family Man spent much of the night listening to the track, "Concrete Jungle," repeatedly. Shakespeare had recorded so many songs, he couldn't remember which he had played on. Finally, the intro jogged his memory.

"Yes, Family, it me who play the bass line."

"Oh yes, no one else could play it but you!"

The next song the Wailers recorded at Harry J's was "Stir It Up." On this track, Bob, the student, surpassed Scratch, his old mentor. Scratch had a love of sexual innuendo in song. But his metaphors could be crude. Bob's managed to be sexy and innocent at the same time. "Stir It Up" never overcooks its sex-as-food theme. Winston "Sparrow" Martin, a studio musician who was recruited to play percussion on the track, says he had heard Johnny Nash's version of the song and he thought it was "too country-western." Martin played his drums quietly on the track because "I wanted to hear the words. Bob's reggae is the deep reggae. I wanted people to hear the Jamaicanness of the song." Bob's lilting delivery, the soothing percussion, and Shakespeare's warm bass line make it all work. Shakespeare recalls that that cut was recorded quickly. He points out: "If you ever been in a session in Jamaica, musicians come up with line quick. Me myself I always have a phrase: 'Take no prisoners.' I used to have to do twenty, thirty, forty songs a day. So I have no time for prisoners. The quicker I can come up with a line, the better." The primary recording for "Stir It Up" was finished in one day.

Sometime later, Shakespeare bumped into Bob walking down Orange Street. Marley paid him "ten or fifteen dollars Jamaican" for his work on the two tracks on *Catch a Fire*. That was less money than Bob had been paid for recording his first single a decade earlier. Shakespeare said the amount didn't really matter to him: "That was the going rate at the time for sessions. You feel nice that you get a money. You feel good."

The day of reckoning had arrived. Blackwell came down to Kingston in late 1972 to hear what the Wailers had recorded. He stopped by the Wailers Record Shack at 127 King Street at the corner of Beeston. He was looking for Bob, Bunny, and Peter. They weren't there. Rita was running the store. Blackwell asked her to pass along the message that he was in town and wanted to hear the record. He told her he was staying at the Skyline Hotel. Blackwell didn't know what he was going to get from the Wailers. He didn't even know if they were going to show up. For the last few weeks, colleagues had kept telling him he was crazy. They said he had thrown his money away by giving the group an advance. But Blackwell remained confident that the trust and respect he had shown the Wailers would be returned.

The next day, Bob, Bunny, and Peter came by in a car to pick up Blackwell at his hotel. They all drove to Harry J's to play him the album. Blackwell recalls he heard only five or six tracks that day. It was enough. One of the songs he heard was "Slave Driver."

The Wailers had conjured the sound Blackwell had dreamed about. The music was intelligent and mysterious. It evoked images of sex and revolution. It seemed to be old music rooted in the folk traditions of the Jamaican countryside, but it also had the insolent swagger of Kingston rude boys. Tears came to his eyes as he listened. Said Blackwell: "When I heard those mixes, it was such a high point for me. It was confirmation that I was right. It was one of the highest points ever for me in my life, obviously . . . hearing the songs and sensing the effort and everything that had gone into it. That money I had given them, it all went in there. You could be clear that they took it really seriously."

Blackwell loved what he heard in Kingston. He loved it so much that he wanted to change it. He felt he had to make it as good as it could possibly be. He flew back to London. Island had started a label for Jamaican music. It had become a rock label. Rock was what was selling. Rock was what the critics respected. Blackwell wanted to turn the Wailers' reggae album into a reggae-rock album.

Bob wasn't happy with the idea of tinkering with what he had created in Jamaica. He was pleased with what he and his bandmates had done. He thought the album was something special. Now he was concerned. He had been cheated and abused by a long line of producers. He wasn't exactly sure what to make of what was happening. Would Blackwell compromise what the Wailers had done? Would he hijack the Wailers' sound as Johnny Nash had done? How could British musicians possibly play reggae? Bob didn't want to leave the album in someone else's control. He flew to England to monitor the album postproduction. He was ready for a fight.

Blackwell, engineer Tony Platt, and Bob began overdubbing and mixing the tracks at Island's Basing Street studio in London near the end of 1972. The dubbing and mixing sessions would start at around 2 P.M. each day and last until 2 A.M. Platt remembers how they progressed: "During the overdub period, Chris popped in and out, but he and I mixed together, although if I remember rightly, I would set the mix up and then we would work it together. Of course there was no automation and so all the balancing and switching had to be a live performance in itself. Naturally, Bob was there all the time during the overdubbing but less so during the mix."

The recordings that the Wailers had delivered to Blackwell included the songs "High Tide or Low Tide," and "All Day All Night." "Usually, when we working, we always do more than enough tracks, more than what we need for the album," Family Man explains. "And then we choose the best, with the strongest lyrics and the best rhythms. When you do an album you don't just do the exact amount, you have to do extras." "High Tide or Low Tide" was an ode to Bob's mother. It could also be read as a tribute to the brotherly devotion the Wailers had shown to one another. Blackwell cut the song from the final album because it sounded too much like the work of an R&B vocal group. "All Day All Night" was a song of passion in which a lover begs his partner for love. Blackwell cut it because, in part, he simply wanted the album to have fewer tracks. "There are nine tracks on *Catch a Fire*," argues Blackwell, "because to me, a ten-track album was a pop album. We wanted songs that had a more extended sense to them. A nine-track album—that's a rock album. That means there's more meat to the music."

Blackwell wanted fewer tracks, but he wanted each track to be longer and weightier. In making reggae more like rock, he felt he was reconnecting Jamaican music to its roots. His view of things: "When Jamaican music started, a lot of it was instrumental, like the people in the Skatalites. There would be solos in early Jamaican music, in ska music. When rock steady and reggae came along, there were no solos. In rock music, there were solos. So what I did is mess with the tape, make a copy of a track, and then edit it and double the length or triple the length. I think with 'Stir It Up,' I tripled the length. So instead of the song structure being a beginning, middle, and end, I'd extend it. I wanted to make it more rockish, more extended, more like rock was, and less like pop."

To flesh out the new, stretched material, Blackwell brought in several American-rock session players. He recruited keyboardist John "Rabbit" Bundrick, who had worked with Bob on his ill-fated soundtrack in Sweden. Bundrick had played with the rock band Free and would go on to work with the Who, Roger Waters of Pink Floyd, and Eric Burdon of the Animals. Rabbit had also played keyboards on Johnny Nash's "I Can See Clearly Now." That song was pop reggae. Marley showed Bundrick how to perform with a roots reggae groove. "What is the most beautiful thing Bob taught me?" Bundrick muses. "The most beautiful thing has to be how to play the 'chink-a-chinka' reggae organ patterns." He would employ what he learned from Bob on such songs as "Slave Driver" and "Kinky Reggae."

Blackwell also brought on board Wayne Perkins, a twenty-year-old guitarist with the American band Smith Perkins Smith. Perkins hailed from Center Point, Alabama. "We are the center of the state," he drawls. "You can't get more southern. You are in the heart of Dixie, pal." When Perkins was growing up, his father played country music by the likes of Hank Williams. His mother had to smuggle R&B albums into the house. "Dad was not a fan of R and B. If he knew we had a turntable and we were playing the N-word music, he would have gone off." Blackwell had signed Smith Perkins Smith to a recording deal with Island. The group's first album had not been a breakthrough and they were working on their second at the Island studios in London. Perkins was eager to stay on Blackwell's good side in order to keep his deal alive.

In the afternoon one day in late 1972, Blackwell stopped Perkins as he was heading down the spiral staircase at Island.

"I've got some Jamaican music here, and I need something different on it," he announced. "I'm wondering if you could put some guitar on it for me?"

"Well, sure," Perkins replied. "What kind of stuff is it?"

"It's kind of got a Latin feel to it, but it's a little different than that. It needs something different."

"What?"

"You know that southern thing you do, that rock-guitar thing you do."

Later that same afternoon, Perkins went down to the recording studio on the lower level of the Island facility that was nicknamed "The Fallout Shelter." Blackwell and Rabbit were there, as was Marley. Blackwell says that he gave the band all the time they needed to complete *Catch a Fire*. But Perkins recalls that at that point in the recording process, all the players were feeling time and monetary pressure. "Marley and them had run out of budget, and they were down to the wire and it was time to make things happen," Perkins claims. "They had all these songs and they still needed a shot in the arm to make things happen." Blackwell had been tinkering with the Wailers' music but hadn't brought out the sonic revelations that he wanted. With every day, success seemed further away rather than closer. Something needed to happen and soon.

Perkins was familiar with reggae. He says he played on at least one track, uncredited, on *The Harder They Come*. (He recorded his part in America.) He felt that Jimmy Cliff's version of reggae on that album was very pop and Americanized. Perkins felt off balance with Bob and his music. He couldn't even understand what Bob was saying because of his Jamaican accent. Laughing, he says: "I lived in England for two years, and when I left there, I could tell you if someone was from Cornwall or Devon or Manchester or Newcastle based on the way they spoke. With Marley it was like he'd come in there, and I'd pick up every third or fourth word, whatever. They had a lot of 'Ire-ike mon! Boom cat! Blot clot!' You don't know what the f—— they're saying!"

The lights were turned down low in the studio. Perkins could make out dreadlocks in the dim lights. It was Bob. He looked like a palm tree silhouetted against the moon. The Fallout Shelter had been transformed into the Caribbean. He could see two white faces in the control room, Blackwell's and Platt's, illuminated by penlights. The smell of herb was in the air. Weird music was pumping out of the speakers.

Perkins spoke into the darkness: "Chris, can you give me a clue as to what's going on here?"

Blackwell shot back: "Well, first off, you forget the bass. The drums are on one and three, you forget the bass—he's a melody guy. Occasionally, he'll play some ones, but you don't rely on him."

"Gotcha. What else can you help with?"

"The keyboards are all on the upbeats."

And with that, they launched into "Concrete Jungle."

Perkins recalls that he had to find his balance quickly: "The very first thing thrown at me was the very first thing you hear on the record ["Concrete Jungle"]. I told Blackwell, look, I play very much from the heart. I am an off-the-top guy, I can't make a chart on this stuff, I don't know where it's going, this is not standard. Everything's backward. The bass and the drums normally are played on the opposite beats. And [in reggae] they come down on the one and the three, as opposed to the two and the four. And I'm playing that backward."

Platt had developed the habit of recording everything so he

could capture spontaneous intros and solos. It paid off in the making of *Catch a Fire*. Perkins says this about the recording of "Concrete Jungle": "So we get going, and I'm sitting here and I'm just diddling around at the front of it, because it takes some time to get into the established beat. I'm playing this weird melody. It's almost like acid music or something and all of a sudden it's established melody." He tried some three runs at the solo. After he finished the third, Platt and Blackwell began celebrating in the control room. Bob, with a wide smile, approached Perkins. Marley had been concerned about Blackwell's meddling, but now he was won over. He gave Perkins his highest accolade—he offered him a puff on his personal spliff. Perkins described the scene: "Everybody started jumping up and down in the control room, and here comes Marley with that big old joint he always carried. I learned how to roll a real one that night. I got high with him. And needless to say, the rest of the night went kind of slow."

It would be a long night. Marley, Blackwell, Platt, and the session players worked from the afternoon until early the next morning. On "Baby We've Got a Date (Rock It Baby)," Perkins played a slide guitar that he hoped would evoke the country blues and Appalachian music he had heard growing up. For the song "Stir It Up," Rabbit played clavinet, Perkins played guitar, and they traded bars, blending the instruments together in a long solo. "They were so experimental for the day," recalls Rabbit about the songs they recorded that night. "We were like mad scientists on those sessions." Bob stayed the entire time, guiding and advising the participants. "He had an air of quiet confidence that somehow set him apart," Platt says. "He struck me as a person I would like to know well but probably never would. I am reminded of this when I read accounts of him from people who claim to have known him well. He had that aspect of loneliness that accompanies genius— perhaps that was part of his magnetic attraction as a performer.

Of course it is easy to romanticize an iconic character such as him and perhaps one should offer the perspective gained from going back and listening to the raw multitracks of 'Stir It Up' and 'Concrete Jungle.' He could sing out of tune just like anyone else."

Around 4 A.M., Perkins left the Fallout Shelter and went upstairs to see if anyone was around. There were still a few stragglers. He packed up his gear and headed home. *Catch a Fire* was done. Perkins said he doesn't recall getting paid for the session: "It might have been a freebie. I think it was."

After the mixing of the album, Blackwell had a final task. He remixed the Wailers' image, starting with the name of the group. Asserts Blackwell: "I knew what I wanted to do. I wanted to change the name from Bob Marley and the Wailers to the Wailers. I wanted to change it to the Wailers because I wanted to present them as a black group." The group needed faces to go with the name. Bob and Peter played guitar and Bunny handled percussion, but the trio had begun as a vocal group. If the Wailers were going to be a band, they needed to have a band. Blackwell asked Marley if there were any Jamaican musicians with whom he was comfortable working. Bob said the Upsetters—Family Man and Carlton Barrett. Blackwell wanted to make them official members of the group—at least when it came to photos. "I said great, let's get them, take a picture with them. So the picture on the back of *Catch a Fire* was taken in London with the five of them, to give the impression of a group, because they weren't really a group at that time."

To further enhance the Wailers' outsider cool, the album sleeve was designed to look like a Zippo lighter. It opened up to reveal a flame. It announced to record buyers that this band was proud to smoke herb—and that they weren't afraid to let things burn. Rod Dyer, who designed the sleeve with Bob Weiner, got the idea for the cover by listening to some tracks from the album. He was taken by the rebellious tone of "Slave Driver." Dyer is a white South African. Disgusted by apartheid, he had moved to America as a young man. He felt as if he could identify with Bob's anger at repressive regimes. Dyer wanted to burn down the old order, too. It struck him that a Zippo lighter would be a good way to start.

The sleeve design was hailed by critics, but it had a practical problem. During shipping, the hinge would break and the top of the lighter would fall off. For the next pressing, Island went with a traditional cover: a close-up image of Bob smoking a spliff. The sexy, intimate photo—Bob is shirtless—was taken by Esther Anderson, a woman with whom Bob would have an affair. Bob had gone from being a rebel to a sex symbol on the same album release. Superstardom had arrived.

Although the Wailers were marketed as a group, Bob was first among equals. Brian Blevins worked in the press office at Island starting in 1972. He was charged with selling the group to the print media. In late 1972, he went down to the studio to meet them as they were finishing *Catch a Fire*. "I had gone down to a mixing session to meet them and let them know that I was working on the press for them," Blevins remembers. "And even though it was the Wailers as a group for the first album, Bob was still the lead person in terms of a media personality. He was really handsome. He had a real spark in his eyes. Although he didn't talk a whole lot, you could sense an aura around him."

Because Blackwell wanted to promote the image of a black group, the two white Americans who had contributed to the album were left off the credits (decades later, their names were included on CD reissues). Complains Perkins: "They still don't want to admit to me being part of that situation. I've never been invited to one Bob Marley festival. I've never played with any of the Wailers. [Marley] might have wanted me in the band if Blackwell would have gone along with it. He knew how to sell records, Chris Blackwell. He knew what it took to sell records. And that was the focal point. And so that's what he did. Who am I to argue with him? The guy's got a 707, for God's sake. He's flying around whenever he wants."

Blackwell realized there was a hunger for authenticity on the part of the record-buying public. White audiences wanted reggae that had the rough edge of rock. But they didn't want black music that seemed like it was trying to pass for white. It was a paradox. The Wailers solved it. Their music made concessions to the marketplace. But they were so cool, so confident, that their credentials could not be challenged. The band that had played "Trench Town Rock" was able to segue painlessly into the world of rock and roll. "The idea of Chris's to combine the reggae with rock players was naturally intriguing and proved to be very exciting," Platt states. "I was also impressed with how natural Bob was and his capacity to embrace the idea and make it his own style."

Reggae attracted new listeners by drawing on the sonic power of rock and emphasizing that the two musical forms shared the same rebel spirit. The Wailers sang of how the "table is turned," dressed in army jackets, and openly smoked ganja. They didn't need rockers to teach them how to be revolutionaries. They hailed from a country that had been fighting for its freedom for hundreds of years. Their authentic insurgent attitude appealed to rockers. Many punk bands, including the Clash, tapped into the reggae beat. (Marley paid tribute to the confluence of punk and reggae on his 1977 song "Punky Reggae Party.") The greatest singer-songwriters in rock and R&B—Bob Dylan, Stevie Wonder, the Beatles, Paul Simon, and others—have recorded songs that draw on reggae rhythms. One might argue that those were simply temporary stylistic sidetracks. But reggae has made other inroads in rap, rock, and elsewhere. The reggae sound has wound its way into a variety of musical genres around the world, from garage to reggaeton. In the 1700s, Maroon warriors in Jamaica, led by three brothers, had fought the British Empire to a draw. In the 1900s, three brothers from Trench Town took on British rock, and conquered the musical world.

Multiculturalism is a weak word. It has too many syllables to be tough. It rhymes with liberalism and conservatism. It conjures images of a mocha-colored future in which books like *Huckleberry Finn* aren't read and deep social divisions aren't fully confronted. Bob made being multicultural not an act of compliance, but an act of defiance. As the planet's cultures blend, Marley's status as a visionary will only rise. Marcus Garvey once told his followers: "Insist on a campaign of race purity . . . and close ranks against all other races. It is . . . a disgrace to mix up your race with other races." Some Rasta meetings in the early 1950s would feature the following chant: "The white man tells us we are inferior. But we know that we are not inferior. We are superior, and he is inferior." Bob had a broader social vision. He believed he was a mix of two cultures. It wouldn't make sense for him to declare civil war on himself. "Me, personally, me can't be prejudice," he said. "Me can't think about life that way because me figure if you're prejudice, that means you have a hate. If you have a hate inside of you, you can't be righteous."

Blending reggae and rock fit in with Bob's musical philosophy. Race had divided his family. Race had divided Jamaica. Race had divided music. Race had divided the world. Bob wanted his music to bring it all back together again. Said Bob: "Music as far as me is family, and just how people tend to break music apart that's how them live. So music shouldn't really be a thing that scatter scatter that much, that reggae have a different root, 'cos all man have one root. That mean people's mind scatter and them think music scatter, too. If the peoples was together them woulda realize that all music is family." He found there was no contradiction in being proud of his heritage and resisting racial categorization.

Catch a Fire was released in America on April 13, 1973. The album was not an instant bestseller, but it drew rave reviews from the music press in the United States and the U.K. Hipsters crowded in to see the Wailers' shows at London's Speakeasy Club. The Island press offices were inundated with interview requests. Bob would go on to become an international icon of revolution and freedom. In 2000, *Time* magazine named Bob Marley and the Wailers' 1977 album *Exodus* as the album of the twentieth century. (Jimi Hendrix's *Are You Experienced?* and Miles Davis's *Kind of Blue* were runners-up.) That same year, the BBC picked "One Love" as the song of the century and the *New York Times* named Marley's 1984 greatest-hits collection, *Legend*, one of the twenty-five greatest albums of the twentieth century. But despite these accolades, Marley remains an outsider figure. He has never appeared on the cover of *Time* magazine. There has never been a dramatic movie based on his life. Jamaica has not declared him a national hero.

As Marley's legend grew after *Catch a Fire*, he retreated. His responses to questions grew less detailed (and they had been spare from the start). He became less clear about the dates of major events in his career. (Perhaps it was the near-constant ganja smoking.) He stopped talking as much about his father and mother. Sometimes he would spin out personal mythology. "My background is my parents is from Africa," he once said. He spoke less about his early days in the music business in Jamaica. He focused more on the music at hand. After *Catch a Fire*, the Wailers quickly began work on their follow-up album. It would be titled *Burnin'*. During the mixing sessions for that record, a British journalist stopped by to interview Bob in the studio. The reporter asked particularly long and weak questions. Bob offered the journalist a pull on his "personal" spliff. The man accepted and took a couple of very deep hits. Bob's spliff was not made from English hash. It was composed of potent Jamaican herb. The reporter's questions soon dissipated in wisps of smoke. The man sank back in a daze. Bob flashed his fellow Wailers a smile. The reggae great took back his spliff. Then Nesta Robert Marley vanished in the haze, like the hills around Nine Miles on a misty morning.

ACKNOWLEDGMENTS

Many of Bob Marley's friends, family members, and bandmates helped me produce this biography. They gave me their time, their insights, and documents relating to Bob. They were there for me "All Day All Night." I talked to more than a hundred sources, but I focused on people who actually knew Bob intimately—who worked with him, lived with him, and made music with him.

I could not have written this book without the advice and assistance of the following people: Bunny Wailer, Chris Blackwell, Rita Marley, Lee "Scratch" Perry, Aston "Family Man" Barrett, Cedella Marley Booker, Cedella Marley, Alan "Skill" Cole, Robbie Shakespeare, Danny Sims, Cherry Green, John "Rabbit" Bundrick, Wayne Perkins, Marcia Griffiths, Winston "Sparrow" Martin, Ernest Ranglin, Toots Hibbert, Cindy Breakspeare, Christopher Marley, Robert Marley, Kate Simon, Tony Platt, Diane Jobson, Brian Jobson, Wayne Jobson, Dickie Jobson, Andy Clayton of wailers.co.uk, Marco Virgona from bobmarleymagazine.com, Kathy Marley-Ames, James Marlow, Perry Henzell, and Justine

Henzell. The following folks were also helpful: Tara Harper, Maria Grahn-Farley, Darby Dunn, Kwame Dawes, Ben Jealous, and my aunt Rosalie. I'd also like to thank my agent, Caron K; my editor, Dawn Davis, and her assistant, Morgan Welebir; my parents, Dr. Rawle Farley and Dr. Ena Farley; my brothers, Anthony, Felipe, and Jonathan; my Caribbean travel companions, Rick and Erin Borovoy; and for helping me readjust to working life after the completion of this book, my colleagues at the *Wall Street Journal*, John Edwards, Shelly Branch, Heather Won Tesoriero, and Melinda Beck. I'm also indebted to the novelist Marguerite Duras for inspiring the first sentence of the last chapter.

BIBLIOGRAPHY

BOOKS

Barrett, Leonard E., Sr. *The Rastafarians*. Beacon, 1988.

Barron, Frank, Alfonso Montouri, and Anthea Barron, eds. *Creators on Creating*. Tarcher, 1997.

Barrow, Steve, and Peter Dalton. *Reggae: The Rough Guide*. The Rough Guides, 1997.

Beckwith, Martha. *Black Roadways: A Study of Jamaican Folklife*. University of North Carolina Press, 1929.

Bethel, E. Clement. *Junkanoo*. Macmillan Education Ltd., 1991.

Black, Clinton V. *History of Jamaica*. Longman Caribbean, 1983.

Blake, Judith. *Family Structure in Jamaica*. The Free Press of Glencove, 1961.

Booker, Cedella Marley. *Bob Marley, My Son*. Taylor Trade Publishing, 2003.

Boot, Adrian, and Chris Salewicz. *Reggae Explosion: The Story of Jamaican Music*. Harry N. Abrams, 2001.

Bradley, Lloyd. *Bass Culture: When Reggae Was King*. Penguin, 2001.

———. *This Is Reggae Music: The Story of Jamaica's Music*. Grove Press, 2000.

Braithwaite, Edward Kamau. *Folk Culture of the Slaves in Jamaica*. New Beacon Books, 1971.

Brody, Eugene B. *Sex, Contraception and Motherhood in Jamaica*. Harvard University Press, 1981.

Caranfa, Angelo. *Camille Claudel: A Sculptor of Interior Solitude*. Bucknell University Press, 1999.

Carey, Bev. *The Maroon Story*. Agouti Press, 1997.

Chevannes, Barry, ed. *Rastafari and Other African-Caribbean Worldviews*. Rutgers University Press, 1998.

Cumbo, Fikisha. *Get Up! Stand Up!* CACE International, 2001.

Cooper, Carolyn. *Noises in the Blood*. Duke University Press, 1995.

Davis, Stephen. *Bob Marley*. Schenkman Books, 1983.

Dawes, Kwame. *Bob Marley: Lyrical Genius*. Sanctuary, 2002.

Defoe, Daniel. *A General History of the Robberies and Murders of the Most Notorious Pirates*. Carroll & Graf, 1999.

De Koningh, Michael, and Laurence Cane-Honeysett. *Young, Gifted and Black: The Story of Trojan Records*. Sanctuary, 2003.

Farley, Rawle. *The Economics of Latin America: Development Problems in Perspective*. Harper & Row, 1972.

———. *Nationalism and Industrial Development in the British Caribbean*. Daily Chronicle, 1958.

Fermor, Patrick Leigh. *The Traveller's Tree: Island Hopping Through the Caribbean in the 1940s*. The Narrative Press, 2004.

Fleming, Ian. *Ian Fleming Introduces Jamaica*. Andre Deutsch Ltd., 1965.

Foehr, Stephen. *Jamaican Warriors: Reggae, Roots and Culture*. Sanctuary, 2000.

Forsythe, Dennis. *Rastafari*. One Drop Books, 1999.

Ghiselin, Brewster, ed. *The Creative Process: A Symposium*. University of California Press, 1952.

Gilroy, Paul. *There Ain't No Black in the Union Jack*. University of Chicago Press, 1991.

Gooden, Lou. *Reggae Heritage*. Oliver Printery, 2003.

Gottlieb, Karla. *The Mother of Us All*. Africa World Press, 2000.

Graves, Joseph L., Jr. *The Emperor's New Clothes: Biological Theories of Race at the Millennium*. Rutgers University Press, 2003.

Gray, Obika. *Radicalism and Social Change in Jamaica, 1960–1972*. The University of Tennessee Press, 1991.

Guerrilla Girls. *The Guerrilla Girls' Bedside Companion to the History of Western Art*. Penguin, 1998.

Haskins, James. *One Love, One Heart: A History of Reggae*. Jump at the Sun/Hyperion, 2002.

Henriques, Fernando. *Family and Colour in Jamaica*. Macgibbon and Kee, 1953.

Howard, David. *Kingston: Cities of the Imagination*. Signal Books/Ian Randle Publishers, 2005.

Hurston, Zora Neale. *Tell My Horse: Voodoo and Life in Haiti and Jamaica*. Perennial, 1990.

Jacobs, H. P. *A Short History of Kingston*. Ministry of Education Publications Branch, 1976.

James, William. *The Principles of Psychology*. Harvard University Press, 1981.

Johnson, Anthony. *Ocho Rios, St. Ann: Portrait of the Garden Parish*. Teejay Ltd., 1995.

Jones, Allan. *Melody Maker: Classic Rock Interviews*. Mandarin, 1994.

Katz, David. *People Funny Boy: The Genius of Lee "Scratch" Perry*. Payback Press, 2000.

———. *Solid Foundation: An Oral History of Reggae*. Bloomsbury, 2003.

King, Stephen A. *Reggae, Rastafari, and the Rhetoric of Social Control*. University Press of Mississippi, 2002.

Lazell, Barry. *Bob Marley: The Illustrated Legend, 1945–1981*. Hamlyn, 1994.

Lee, Helene. *The First Rasta*. Lawrence Hill Books, 1999.

Lewin, Olive. *Rock It Come Over: The Folk Music of Jamaica*. University of the West Indies Press, 2000.

Lewis, William F. *Soul Rebels: The Rastafari*. Waveland Press, 1993.

Lowe, Henry, and Errol Morrison *Marijuana, Cannabis, Ganja: The Jamaican Connection*. Pelican Publishers, 2001.

Lunita, Karl. *Jamaica Handbook*. Moon Travel Handbooks, 2000.

Malraux, André. *The Voices of Silence: Man and His Art*. Translated by Stuart Gilbert. Doubleday & Company, 1953.

Marcus, Harold G. *Haile Selassie I: The Formative Years, 1892–1936*. The Red Sea Press, 1996.

Marley, Cedella. *The Boy from Nine Miles: The Early Life of Bob Marley*. Hampton Roads, 2002.

Marley, Rita. *No Woman No Cry*. Hyperion, 2004.

Marley, Rita, with Adrian Boot and Chris Salewicz. *Bob Marley: Songs of Freedom*. Viking Studio Books, 1992.

Martin, Tony. *Literary Garveyism*. TM Press, 1983.

Mastalia, Francesco, Alfonse Pagano, and Alice Walker. *Dreads*. Artisan, 1999.

McCann, Ian. *Bob Marley: In His Own Words*. Omnibus Press, 1993.

McCann, Ian, and Harry Hawke. *Bob Marley: The Complete Guide to His Music*. Omnibus Press, 2004.

Murrell, Nathaniel Samuel, William David Spencer, and Adrian Anthony McFarlane. *Chanting Down Babylon*. Temple, 1998.

Nahm, Milton. *The Artist as Creator*. Johns Hopkins Press, 1956.

Parker, Rozsika, and Griselda Pollock. *Old Mistresses*. Pantheon, 1981.

Paton, Diana. *No Bond But the Law: Punishment, Race, and Gender in Jamaican State Formation, 1780–1870*. Duke University Press, 2004.

Philpott, Don. *Landmark Visitors Guide: Jamaica*. Hunter Publishing, 1993.

Pollard, Velma. *Dread Talk: The Language of the Rastafari*. Canoe Press, 1994.

Potash, Chris. *Reggae, Rasta, Revolution*. Schirmer Books, 1997.

Robinson, Carey. *The Fighting Maroons of Jamaica*. Collins & Sangster, 1969.

Selassie, Haile. *My Life and Ethiopia's Progress. Volume I: 1892–1937*. Frontline Distribution International, 1999.

Senior, Olive. *Encyclopedia of Jamaican Heritage*. Twin Guinep Publishers, 2003.

Sheff, David. *All We Are Saying*. St. Martin's, 2000.

Sheridan, Maureen. *Soul Rebel*. Thunder's Mouth Press, 1999.

Sherlock, Philip, and Hazel Bennett. *The Story of the Jamaican People*. Ian Randle Publishers, 1998.

Smith, Honor Ford. "Lionheart Gal: Life Stories of Jamaican Women." The Women's Press, 1986.

Sobo, Elisa Janine. *One Blood: The Jamaican Body*. SUNY Press, 1993.

Steffens, Roger, and Leroy Jodie Pierson. *Bob Marley and the Wailers: The Definitive Discography*. Rounder Books, 2005.

Stolzoff, Norman C. *Wake the Town and Tell the People: Dancehall Culture in Jamaica*. Duke University Press, 2000.

Taylor, Don. *Marley and Me: The Real Bob Marley Story*. Barricade Books, 1995.

Various authors. *The Gleaner: Geography and History of Jamaica*, 24th edition. The Gleaner Company, 1995.

Various authors. *Insight Guide Jamaica*. APA Publications.

Ward, Ned. *A Trip to Jamaica: With a True Character of the People and the Island*. 1698.

White, Timothy. *Catch a Fire: The Life of Bob Marley*. Owl Books, 1983.

Whitney, Malika Lee, and Dermott Hussey. *Bob Marley: Reggae King of the World*. Pomegranate Artbooks, 1984.

Wint, Eleanor, and Carolyn Cooper. *Bob Marley: The Man and His Music*. Arawak Publications, 2003.

PERIODICALS

The Aquarian. "Peter Tosh: A State-of-the-Art Urban Rasta," by Richard Grabel. April 25, 1979.

The Beat. "Bob's Delaware Days," by Roger Steffens. Vol. 12, No. 3.

The Beat. "Bob Marley Raps It Up in Boston," by Larry Katz. Vol. 10, No. 3, 1991.

The Beat. "Bob Marley: Talkin' Revolution," by Richard Cromelin. Vol. 14, No. 3, 1995.

The Beat. "The Beverly Kelso Story: Songbird of Simmer Down," by Timothy White. Vol. 10, No. 3, 1991.

The Beat. "Beverly Kelso: The Lost Voice of the Wailers," by Roger Steffens, Vol. 23, No. 3, 2004.

The Beat. "A Conversation with Rita Marley." Vol. 10, No. 3.

The Beat. "First Fruits: Original Wailer Cherry Green." Vol. 23, No. 3, 2004.

The Beat. "In the Beginning: Mr. Dodd Coxson," by Roger Steffens. Vol. 13, No. 3, 1994.

The Beat. "Joe Higgs: In His Own Words," by Roger Steffens. Vol. 19, No. 1.

The Beat. "High Tide or Low Tide: Dr. Gayle McGarrity," interview by Roger Steffens. Vol. 20, No. 3, 2001.

The Beat. Interview with Bob Marley. Vol. 19, No. 3.

The Beat. "Roots Natty Roots," 1975 Interview with Bob Marley, by Rob Bowman. Vol. 16, No. 3, 1997.

The Beat. "Vision Walker." Vol. 14, No. 3, 1995.

Black Music. "Let Herb Be Free," by Carl Gayle. September 1976.

Black Music. "Marley Speaks," by Roy Coleman. June 1976.

Black Music & Jazz Review. "Bob Marley—Return of the Native," by Chris May. April 1978.

Black Music & Jazz Review. "The Struggle Continues," by Chris May. May 1983.

Caribbean Today. February 28, 1994.

Circus. "A Puff Away from Huge," by Fred Schruers. July 6, 1978.

Crawdaddy. "Bob Marley's Jamaica," by Timothy White. January 1976.

Creem. "Bob Marley Battles De Blood Clot, Mon," by Rob Patterson. July 1978.

Creem. "Peter Tosh: He's the Toughest," by Barbara Charone. March 1979.

Daily Gleaner. "Bob Raped Me!" April 1, 2004.

Daily Gleaner. "Celebrations in Rural Areas." August 10, 1962.

Daily Gleaner. "Cindy Comes In Quietly." December 27, 1976.

Daily Gleaner. "How the Parishes Celebrated." August 9, 1962.

Daily Gleaner. "It Seems to Me," by Peter Simple. June 15, 1951.

Daily Gleaner. "Kingston Remains Music City." April 11, 1978.

Daily Gleaner. "Tonight! Tonight!" October 9, 1965.

Everybody's Magazine. "Mrs. Cedella Booker, Bob Marley's Mother." July 10, 1982.

Everybody's Magazine. "Marley Speaks." June/July 1978.

Everybody's Magazine. "One Final Major Interview." September 18, 1980.

Flair Magazine. "Bob Marley's and Bunny Wailer's Secret Sister." April 2, 1990.

The Gleaner. "May Visit Island." December 30, 1929.

The Gleaner Sunday Magazine. "Marley Gives His Views." March 11, 1979.

High Times. "Captured: Peter Tosh Dread and Alive," by John Swenson. November 1981.

Hit Parader. "The Hit Parader Interview: Bob Marley," by David Rensin. September 1976.

High Times. "Peter Tosh and Bunny Wailer," by Bagga Brown. April 1983.

High Times. "The Rastafarians," by J. B. Alexander. October/November 1975.

Hit Parader. "The Wailers," by Lenny Kaye. July 1974.

Hit Parader. "We Play the Music We Want," by Joseph Rose. April 1977.

Honey. "Bob Marley," by Moyra Ashford. November 1975.

Impressions: Magazine of the Arts. "Bob Marley," by Bob Bryan. 1975.

The Independent. May 7, 2004.

Jamaica Daily News. "Bob Lets It All Hang Out." September 5, 1975.

Jamaica Gleaner. "What's in a Name?" Undated article.

Jamaica Gleaner. "Court Admonishes Rastafari Men." June 9, 1950.

Jamaica Observer. "From Broadway to Kingston: The Story of Danny Sims and the Wailers," by Howard Campbell. February 15, 2004.

Jamaica Observer. "Sir Coxsone Dodd Is Dead," by Balford Henry. May 5, 2004.

L.A. Free Press. Interview with Wanda Coleman, December 1973.

Let It Rock, "Jimmy Cliff, Interviewed by Charlie Gillett," November 1972.

Let It Rock. "The Wailers and the New Reggae," by Carl Gayle. July 1973.

Mojo. "10 Questions for Lee 'Scratch' Perry," by Lloyd Bradley. July 2003.

Mojo. "The Folk Singer," by Chris Salewicz. March 1995.

Melody Maker. "In the Studio with the Wailers," by Richard Williams. June 23, 1973.

Melody Maker. "The First Genius of Reggae?" by Richard Williams, February 24, 1973.

New Musical Express. "The Kook," by Stefan De Batselier. July 26, 1997.

New Musical Express. "Marley: Don't Deal with Dark Things . . ." by Ray Coleman. June 12, 1976.

New Musical Express. "Me Just Wanna Live, Y'unnerstan?" by Neil Spencer. July 19, 1975.

New Musical Express. "Rastafari Rock," by Sebastian Clarke. May 12, 1973.

People. "For a Song," by Lee Wohlfert. April 26, 1976.

People. "Three Years After Bob's Death," by Jonathan Cooper. November 19, 1984.

People. "You Can Get It If You Really Want." May 24, 1982.

Philadelphia Daily News. August 4, 1995.

Reggae Report. "All About Cousin Bob," by Deanne Lucy. Vol. 10, No. 4, 1992.

Reggae Report. "Cedella Marley Booker Celebrates Bob Marley Day in Toronto," by Sharain Santalla. Vol. 10, No. 4, 1992.

Reggae Report. "Exclusive 1977 Bob Marley Interview," by Jeff Cathrow with Eugenia Polos. Vol. 7, No. 4, 1989.

Reggae Report. "Joe Higgs: The Teacher Then and Now," by Lee O'Neill. Vol. 12, No. 7, 1995.

Reggae Report. "Peter Tosh," by Terri Larsen. Vol. 7, 1989.

Reggae News. "Reasoning with Tosh," by Hank Holmes and Roger Steffens. Vol. 2, Nos. 3 and 4.

Rock and Folk Magazine. "Babylon by Rolls," by Herve Muller, translated by Gael Doyen. 1978.

Rockers. "The "Sen-se-Tional Rita Marley. High on One Draw." Vol. 2, No. 5, 1981.

Select. "Lee Scratch Perry's Mysterious World," by Clark Collis. June 1995.

Smash Hits. "Better off Dread," by Mike Stand. August 7–20, 1980.

Social and Economic Studies. "Sexual Behaviour of Jamaicans: A Literature Review," by Barry Chevannes. Vol. 42, No. 1, March 1993.

Sunday Gleaner. "Al Agog over Cindy." December 5, 1976.

Sunday Gleaner. "Battle of the Greats." June 20, 1965.

Sunday Gleaner. "Coxsone Dodd and His Music," by Claude Mills. April 13, 1995.

Sunday Gleaner. "The Fantastic Bob Marley." August 10, 1975.

Sunday Gleaner. "Jamaican Is Miss Universe." September 19, 1976.

Sunday Gleaner. "The Reggae Rush Is On," by Fitzroy Nation. August 8, 1976.

Uncut. "Catch a Fire," by Nigel Williamson. March 2001.

The Voice. November 25, 1996.

The Washington Post. "Dread Reckoning: The Marley Mess," by Richard Leiby. August 25, 1991.

Zig Zag. "Marley Uprising," by Kris Needs. August 1980.

OTHER MEDIA

African Herbsman, Bob Marley and the Wailers, audio CD 2001.

Arkology, Lee "Scratch" Perry, CD boxed set liner notes, 1997.

"Behind the Smile: The Real Life of Bob Marley," BBC radio documentary, 2005.

The Birth of a Legend, Bob Marley and the Wailers, audio CD, liner notes, 1990.

Bobmarley.com

Bobmarley.freeserve.co.uk

Bob Marley in Philadelphia 1979, interview CD.

Bob Marley in Paris 1980, interview CD.

Burnin', Bob Marley and the Wailers, vinyl album, 1973.

Catch a Fire (Deluxe Edition), Bob Marley and the Wailers, audio CD, 2003.

Catch a Fire, Bob Marley and the Wailers vinyl album, 1973.

Classic Albums: Bob Marley and the Wailers—Catch a Fire, DVD documentary, 2000.

Climb the Ladder, Bob Marley and the Wailers, liner notes, 2000.

The Complete Bob Marley & the Wailers, 1967 to 1972, Part II, CD boxed set liner notes, 1997.

The Complete Upsetters Collection, CD boxed set liner notes, 2002.

Confrontation, Bob Marley and the Wailers, vinyl album, 1983.

Destiny: Rare Ska Sides from Studio One, Bob Marley and the Wailers, liner notes, 1999.

Exodus, vinyl album, 1977.

Going Back to My Roots, 1979 CD interview with Bob Marley.

Greatest Hits at Studio One, Bob Marley and the Wailers, CD liner notes.

Grooving Kingston 12, Bob Marley and the Wailers, CD boxed set liner notes, 2004.

I Am the Upsetter, Lee "Scratch" Perry, boxed CD set liner notes, 2005.

Interview with Jay Strasser on WRUV in Burlington, Vermont, circa 1980.

Interview with Neville Willoughby in Jamaica in 1973.

Interview with Red Ronnie in Milan, Italy, in 1980.

Jamaica Gleaner online, "Pieces of the Past" series.

Junior Braithwaite, phone interview with Roger Steffens, May 5, 1985.

Kaya, Bob Marley and the Wailers, vinyl album, 1978.

London Press Conference with Bob Marley, July 17, 1975.

Natty Dread, vinyl album, 1975.

"Old Fire Sticks" by Roger Steffens, from the Reggae Festival Guide On-line.

"One Day France Will Be Africa," Bob Marley interview with Patrick Barrat, Tuff Gong, Jamaica, 1980.

Rastaman Vibration, vinyl album, 1976.

Rasta Revolution, Bob Marley and the Wailers, audio CD, 2001.

Rebel Music: The Bob Marley Story, DVD documentary, 2001.

Santa Barbara press conference with Bob Marley, 1979.

Simmer Down at Studio One, Bob Marley and the Wailers, CD liner notes, 1994.

Songs of Freedom, Bob Marley and the Wailers, CD boxed set liner notes, 1999.

Soul Almighty: The Formative Years, Vol. I, Bob Marley, audio CD, 1996.

Soul Rebel, Bob Marley and the Wailers, audio CD, 2002.

Stepping Razor: Red X, DVD documentary, 2000.

The Studio One Story, DVD set, Soul Jazz Records, 2002.

Survival, Bob Marley and the Wailers, vinyl album, 1979.

This Is Reggae Music: The Golden Era, 1960–1975, CD boxed set liner notes, 2004.

Tougher Than Tough: The Story of Jamaican Music, boxed set liner notes, 1993.

Uprising, Bob Marley and the Wailers, vinyl album, 1980.

The Wailers Legacy, Bunny Wailer, limited edition CD boxed set, 2004.

World Factbook: Jamaica People

CHRISTOPHER JOHN FARLEY was born in Kingston, Jamaica, and raised in Brockport, New York. He is a graduate of Harvard University and a former editor of the *Harvard Lampoon*. He is the author of the bestselling biography *Aaliyah: More Than a Woman* and the novels *My Favorite War* and *Kingston by Starlight*. He is also the coauthor of *Martin Scorsese Presents the Blues*. He has worked as an editor and pop music critic at *Time* magazine and is currently an editor at the *Wall Street Journal*.